Dear Dave,

I am truly grateful for your support. I truly means a lot an wait to see what you to accomplish in life. All a

The Will of Heroes

The Proven Path to Greatness That Anyone Can Follow

Colin Robertson

Willpowered⚡

Printed in the United States of America

ISBN: 978-0-9973631-1-1

Willpowered Inc
5410 29th Ave S.
Gulfport, FL 33707

www.willpowered.co

Contents

To Liz, Jeff, Brianna, and everyone who pledged their support in order to make this book a reality.

Part I

The Power of Will

Introduction

The Will of a Hero

"I can't relate to lazy people. I don't understand you. I don't want to understand you."

– Kobe Bryant

When he was twelve years old, Kobe Bryant was about to give up basketball forever. He had just completed his summer basketball camp and was going home a disgrace. He'd thought it would be the beginning of a flawless journey to becoming the star National Basketball Association (NBA) player that we all know today—especially because his father, Joe Bryant, played in the NBA for eight years before playing his final six years in Italy.

During those six years abroad, the Bryant family had fully embraced the Italian culture. That included Kobe playing soccer for most of his youth and showing a lot of promise in the sport. But in the summer of 1991, his family moved back to America, and he finally had a chance to play his father's favorite game.

He entered the camp and played against some of the most talented youngsters in the country—and they embarrassed him. Kobe did not score a single point. Not one jumper, not one layup, not one free throw. Nothing. He spent that entire summer in frustration, questioning whether basketball was really for him. He was, after all, a promising soccer player—so why dream of becoming a basketball player when he clearly had no talent for it?

Then Kobe read about one of his heroes, Michael Jordan. He learned how Michael got cut from his high school basketball team, but didn't quit. Getting cut motivated Michael to outwork everyone around him to prove his coach wrong. When Kobe learned this, it created a fire inside of him that would never be put out. He wanted to work harder than everyone else for the rest of his basketball career—and he did.

When Kobe entered high school, he got to the gym every morning at five o'clock and would not leave the afternoon practice until seven in the evening. After the official practice was over, he convinced his high school teammates to play one-on-one games with him, sometimes up to 100 points. He singled out any players who could help him improve his skills and forced them to challenge him. His relentless work ethic over his high school career turned him into one of the best players in the country. He was so good, in fact, that six years after he failed to score a single point in basketball camp, Kobe was drafted thirteenth overall in the NBA.

But his work ethic didn't stop there. He continued to push himself even harder as an NBA player. He practiced by himself—sometimes even without a ball—hours before his teammates showed up at the gym. He forced himself to make 400 shots every single practice. He put himself through four hours of intense workouts on game days. He stopped eating sugar and followed one of the strictest diets in the NBA. And he continued to ask teammates to stay after practice to face him one on one. Some NBA players love to play under the bright lights of the arena, but Kobe Bryant loved to put in the work before the lights ever came on...and then stay long after they were turned off.

All of this hard work led Kobe to become a seventeen-time NBA All-Star, a five-time NBA champion, a two-time NBA Finals MVP, and a two-time Olympic gold medalist. All of this happened despite the fact that, as a twelve-year-old boy, he showed the least amount of promise of *anyone* in his basketball camp. Clearly, it was not innate talent that helped Kobe Bryant reach his extraordinary success. It was practice.

Kobe's eventual success in spite of his initial failure proves that if someone followed Kobe's path, he or she could reach the same level of success. There is nothing preventing another boy entering his first year of high school from getting to the gym at five o'clock each morning and practicing until seven o'clock each evening. There is nothing stopping a girl from recognizing areas of weakness in her game and working relentlessly to improve them. There is nothing stopping either from following a strict diet or doing intense four-hour workouts on game days. Nor is there anything stopping them from meticulously counting 400 made shots every single day. All of these practices are within the control of anyone— which means achieving Kobe Bryant's level of success is also within the control of anyone.

So why aren't more people as successful as Kobe Bryant? Because following his path is hard, painful, and boring. To follow it requires something more than simply knowing what to do. It requires the one thing that separates those who achieve greatness from everyone else. It requires *willpower*.

Heroes show you what's possible. They prove that following a certain path can lead to extraordinary success. In this book, you will learn how some of the most successful people of all time, across multiple areas of expertise, developed the willpower to achieve true greatness. You will read about the paths taken by Wolfgang Amadeus Mozart, J.K. Rowling, Warren Buffett, and others like them. You will learn the science behind their achievements from research that explains how willpower actually works and how you can make the most of it in your life. Then you will learn the practical, scientifically proven strategies you can use to develop your willpower and achieve greatness in your own right.

They say greatness is a journey. I hope reading this book will be the beginning of yours!

Chapter 1

The Myth of Talent

"Neither a lofty degree of intelligence, nor imagination, nor both go together in making a genius. Love, love, love—that is the soul of genius."
– Wolfgang Amadeus Mozart

Leopold Mozart knew the thought was preposterous. *Could he really begin teaching his four-year-old son Wolfgang to play the piano?* Wolfgang had been around music all of his life. The Mozart home was always filled with new students being taught by Leopold to play the piano. This included Wolfgang's older sister, Maria Anna, who practiced day and night. This constant exposure to music helped Wolfgang develop a deep love for it.

The same exposure, however, also made Wolfgang jealous. He wanted to learn how to play the piano, just like his sister and the other children who came into the Mozart home. So, for years, he begged his father to teach him. Eventually, Leopold relented and began teaching piano to his son.

Immediately, Leopold could see that there was something different about Wolfgang. He seemed to get completely lost in the music. He was so focused, so absorbed, and so intent on learning—even as a four-year-old. Along with his seemingly superhuman ability to immerse himself in his musical studies, young Wolfgang clearly had another major advantage over his peers: He had an extraordinary passion for all aspects of music.

He loved listening to it, he loved playing it, and he even loved practicing pieces that should have been too difficult for him. When he found a piece that challenged him, Wolfgang would practice it over and over until he was finally able to conquer it. He also loved to improve on the music he played by taking a piece he had mastered and adding his own personal touch to it. Not only was he learning how to play the works of other composers, he was actually beginning to compose music of his own.

Wolfgang continued his consistent practice for two years, at which point Leopold decided he would take Wolfgang, who was now six, and his older sister on a tour of Europe. Wolfgang would dress as a court minister, Maria Anna as a princess, and they would dazzle audiences from Vienna to Paris. So Leopold took his children across the continent, and the crowds could not get enough of the adorable young musicians. Their show was so popular that it was Wolfgang and his sister who supported the Mozart family, not Leopold.

At the extraordinarily young age of six, Wolfgang Amadeus Mozart did not just play music and did not just compose music, but actually performed music at such a high level in concerts across Europe that he was the primary breadwinner for his family. If there has ever been an example of innate talent, Mozart has to be it, right? How else can we explain his remarkable accomplishments at such a young age? In his book *Mastery,* Robert Greene challenged the role of Mozart's talent in his success by examining his story a little more closely.

Talent, or Something Else?

We know that Wolfgang Amadeus Mozart was exposed to music from the moment he entered the world. The music played by Leopold's students filled the Mozart home all day, and the music played by Wolfgang's older sister filled it all night. Although Wolfgang loved the music, he was also jealous of the affection the other children—especially Maria Anna—received from his father. He saw how much her playing impressed their father, and Wolfgang wanted to impress him in the same way. This ignited a passion inside Wolfgang to learn music and gain his father's affection.

So he begged Leopold to teach him. But by the time his father finally began teaching him, Wolfgang was years behind his sister in terms of skill and practice. She was five years older than him, so even though Wolfgang started learning, she was still developing more quickly; a ten-year-old with a year of practice will likely be better at listening to, understanding, and playing music than a five-year-old with the same amount of study. This meant Wolfgang was constantly playing catch-up to win the affection of his father, giving him extra motivation to continue practicing and pushing his limits in order to play as well as his older sister.

This motivation, along with the fact that music was simply a way of life in the Mozart household, led to Wolfgang's deep affection for it. He truly loved music. It was not a chore for him to practice in the way that it was for many other children. In fact, music was actually therapeutic for him.

As a child, Wolfgang had problems with mood swings and a tendency to lash out at others—except when he was fully immersed in music. So, unlike other children his age who would get rid of pent-up energy by playing outside, he would get rid of his pent-up energy by playing piano. Leopold learned to deal with Wolfgang's temper tantrums by placing him in front of the piano with a challenging piece, thereby releasing his anger while also improving his skills.

When the Mozart siblings embarked on their tour across Europe, the crowds who gathered to see young Wolfgang and his sister were not attending primarily for the quality of the music. It was much more about the spectacle. They came to see the precious young children dressed up like adults; theirs were performances about novelty, not purely music. This meant that Wolfgang had the opportunity to get experience performing in front of crowds that were forgiving. In fact, when he or his sister did make a mistake, it was brushed off by the audience because of the performers' young ages.

All of these factors combined to instill in Mozart a passion not only for music, but also for challenging and deliberate practice that made him a better musician. He became capable of filling concert venues all over Europe and putting bread on his family's table—not because he was a professional-caliber musician, but because, at six years old, he was a novelty for audiences. Clearly, it was not pure talent that made the difference for Wolfgang. So what was it?

The Real Determinant of Success

To find out the real determinant of success in any field, psychologist John Hayes looked at how long it took the best composers to create their first great work. He found that nobody—including Wolfgang—had produced a composition of any significance until about ten years after they first took up music. This means that even Wolfgang, who had essentially every advantage when it came to becoming a brilliant musician, still had to practice his skills for a full ten years before creating anything great. No amount of innate talent, even in a field of "genius" such as music, could overcome the years of practice necessary to create a great work. Someone may be talented or may be lucky, but he or she still has to go through ten years of practice in order to become a master.

This finding has been verified many times by other researchers. Anders Ericsson found that in order to achieve expert performance in any field, one must engage in 10,000 hours of deliberate practice. Author Malcolm Gladwell further confirmed this finding in his book *Outliers,* where he discusses the fact that success stories like Bill Gates and the Beatles only started seeing true results after they had reached those 10,000 hours of practice, and Robert Greene also confirmed this rule in more people than Mozart. Benjamin Franklin, Charles Darwin, and many other "masters" in their fields all abided by the 10,000-hour rule. The overwhelming evidence today proves that in order to achieve top-level performance, you must put in at least ten years or 10,000 hours of practice toward a specific skill or domain.

To some, this finding may not make sense. After all, look at our society. There are plenty of people who have studied in a particular field for over ten years or accumulated well over 10,000 hours of work in their domain, yet they have nowhere near the success of a Benjamin Franklin or a Bill Gates. Doesn't this prove that those people had an innate special gift that allowed them to improve *more* from their 10,000 hours than another person would? Perhaps it is not talent alone that makes you great, you might wonder, but isn't that talent what separates you from the rest as long as you are willing to put in the work? These are valid concerns; so let's address them by explaining "deliberate practice."

Deliberate Practice

To explain deliberate practice, psychologist Aubrey Daniels uses an example of two basketball players who are learning how to shoot. The players commit themselves to 100 hours of practice in order to become proficient shooters. For the first hour, Player A takes 200 practice shots and Player B takes 50. Player B retrieves his own shots, dribbles leisurely, and takes several breaks to talk with friends. Meanwhile, Player A has a colleague who retrieves the ball after each of her shots. This colleague also keeps a record of the shots she makes. If Player A misses a shot, her colleague records whether the miss was short, long, left, or right. She reviews the results after every ten minutes of practice to adjust her shots accordingly. Assuming that this is typical of each player's normal practice routine and that they are equally skilled at the start, which person would you predict would be the better shooter after the 100 hours of practice?

This is the difference between top performers and average performers. Top performers spend their time practicing like Player A, and average performers spend their time practicing like Player B. Wolfgang improved because he was constantly challenging himself. He was striving to get better at all times. He also received consistent feedback from Leopold, who had the skill and authority to help guide Wolfgang's development. These factors, as well as his deep passion for his field, are the reasons why he was able to perform at such a high level—not because of some innate gift.

There are three key components that separate deliberate practice from average practice:

1) *Improve your weaknesses, not your strengths.* Doing things that we are good at is fun. We get a lot of enjoyment out of showing off our skills, even if we are only showing them off to ourselves. But Wolfgang did not seek to equal his sister's skills by playing music he could already play beautifully. He did it by finding pieces that challenged him. Kobe Bryant, too, did not get better by showing off his skills to his teammates. He found teammates who were great in an area, like being a lockdown defender, and practiced against their strength until he learned to defeat it. He never chose players he could dominate; he chose players who could give him a legitimate challenge. He wasn't practicing to show off; he was practicing to improve every aspect of his game.

In your domain, you must find a way to challenge yourself in the areas in which you need improvement. Whatever skill you are trying to master, see how you can isolate certain areas of it and begin challenging yourself in a way that will force you to improve. If your skill is sales, for example, you might be great with people but poor at organization. So rather than practicing sales calls, practice organizing information about potential clients, like their budgets, concerns, and important dates. As you continue to isolate your weaknesses and improve them, you will begin to see extraordinary improvement in your overall ability.

2) *Get consistent feedback.* Leopold Mozart was not only valuable because he could guide Wolfgang's development, but also because he could provide constant feedback. He could see where Wolfgang was struggling and instruct him on how to improve. This kind of feedback does not necessarily require another person. Kobe Bryant gets consistent feedback from the basketball hoop. If he takes a bad shot, he can see where he missed and correct the error for his next shot. The important thing is to simply have the opportunity to make an attempt, get feedback on it, and then adjust accordingly.

Feedback is where many people fail when it comes to designing their deliberate practice. Practicing your work without feedback is like bowling without any pins. Without feedback of some kind, you cannot learn how to adjust and improve. In your practice, see if there is someone who is willing to give you feedback on your work. This person does not need to be a coach, a mentor, or even a person with more skill than you. Usually, you simply need a different perspective. Kobe Bryant, for example, is a better basketball player than any coach he has played for. But he listens to his coaches because they can see his practice differently. If you cannot find someone to give you feedback, see if you can design your own feedback system. It doesn't matter *how* you get your feedback; it just matters that you do get it.

3) *Make the process repeatable.* Wolfgang did not get all of his practice done in one sitting. He played pieces over and over again until he had them mastered. Kobe forced himself to make 400 shots every single day. In order to improve their

weaknesses, these heroes were willing to try over and over again until they got it right. They went through their practice repetitions until the new skill was second nature for them.

You will never learn a new skill in your domain by going through the process once. Someone who is practicing her skills in investing will not learn anything by choosing one stock. She must invest in several things, adjust based on the feedback of the market, and repeat. Find a way to make your own practice highly repeatable. Then continue the repetitions until your new skill is second nature.

The Result of Deliberate Practice

At the age of twenty-five, Wolfgang was a truly masterful musician. He composed music with such elegance that he felt as if he were seducing the audience with each note. He had been practicing for over twenty years and produced some of the greatest compositions the world has ever seen—even to today.

But he still didn't have the creative freedom to do as he pleased. He was employed as a court musician under the Archbishop of Salzburg, who treated him as if he were simply average. Leopold, too, expected Wolfgang to follow his orders. After all, where would Wolfgang be were it not for his instruction?

Eventually, the two of them could not keep the creative fire inside Wolfgang from bubbling to the surface. He no longer wanted to work as a court musician and take instruction from his father; he was ready to go off and create a legacy of his own. So Wolfgang retired from his position as a court musician and completely cut ties with his father.

After making the decision to go off on his own, Wolfgang exploded. He had been practicing music for twenty years and could now think on an entirely different musical level than anyone before him. He had experience in almost every genre of music and could compose a symphony as well as he could compose an opera. And now that he had the creative freedom to do as he pleased, he spent the remainder of his short life composing at a feverish pace. In the end, he composed over 600 works, including 50 symphonies, 25 piano concertos, and 21 operas.

True greatness takes time. Even Wolfgang did not produce his greatest work until twenty years after first learning how to play the piano. But because he was persistent with his deliberate practice, he changed the world with his music. And he will forever be remembered as the genius of geniuses—not because he was born a genius, but because he had the will to continue practicing until he *became* a genius.

Deliberate practice is hard. It is frustrating. It is boring. But Wolfgang's story proves that if you have the willpower to endure all of that, then your results will be spectacular. Greatness is not born. Greatness is built—day by day, practice by practice, hour by hour.

Conclusion

The story of Wolfgang Amadeus Mozart is often cited as "proof" that there is such a thing as innate talent. He supposedly demonstrates that some of us are simply born with the ability to play a musical instrument, write, or be an athlete. When you examine the Mozart story, however, you can see how many other factors were in place to help Wolfgang develop into a brilliant musician. He still had to endure over ten years of deliberate practice in order to produce a great piece of music.

Deliberate practice involves working on your weaknesses, getting consistent feedback, adjusting based on what you learned, and repeating the process until it is second nature. The overwhelming scientific evidence shows that if you can maintain this practice for ten years or 10,000 hours, you can attain mastery in any field. But deliberate practice is hard, frustrating, and boring.

You must develop the willpower to endure this practice—and that is what the rest of this book is all about.

Key Points

- *Talent is overrated.* Seen through a scientific lens, researchers have found a consistent pattern of reaching great performance that has nothing to do with innate gifts or talent. No one who truly achieves greatness does so until he or she has accomplished at least ten years or 10,000 hours of deliberate practice.

- *Deliberate practice is different than average practice.* Deliberate practice is about more than simply working hard or spending time doing something. It is more focused, challenging, and designed for consistent improvement.

Strategies

1) *Improve your weaknesses, not your strengths.* Find the things you need to work on within your field, and focus on improving them.

2) *Get consistent feedback.* Try to find a mentor, friend, coach, or some other mechanism to give you feedback on your work. You can't improve if you don't know why you made a mistake in the first place.

3) *Making the process highly repeatable.* Improvement comes through long-term repetition. Find a way to practice your craft on a daily basis.

Part II

Understanding and Increasing Willpower

Chapter 2

Understanding Your Willpower

"Put one foot in front of the other. Focus on the little goal right in front of you, and almost anything is possible."
– Joe De Sena

Joe De Sena woke up in a daze. Everything had happened so fast. One minute he was driving with his best friend; then the next thing he knew he was waking up in a hospital bed, learning that he had been in a terrible accident—an accident so bad that his hip had been ripped out of its socket.

After his injury, the first four doctors Joe met with said that he would never run again. This news devastated Joe. He'd been an athlete and a fierce competitor all of his life and could not imagine never running again.

So Joe refused to accept that fate. He became hyper-focused. He decided that he was going to do everything he could to run again. He was going to prove doctors wrong, prove that his will was unbreakable.

To get back to running, he followed a strict rehab program, starting small with Pilates and slowly but surely improving his ability to walk. He had to push through the pain of rehab every single day, but he was so focused, so committed, and so willing to do anything to run again that by the end of the year, he wasn't just running—he had crushed fourteen Ironman triathlons.

Since then, Joe has run over 100 endurance races, including more than 25 Ironmans, a 100-mile ultramarathon, and even-harder adventure races that lasted multiple days in conditions so harsh that competitors lost toes, limbs, and even their lives. And

Joe was doing all of it with a body that doctors had thought was incapable of running again.

But being an athlete is only part of Joe's story. While he was defying doctors and his own physical limitations, he was also building a company that has helped over a million people defy their limitations as well: Spartan Race. Joe pioneered the concept in 2009, and "obstacle course racing," as it would later be called, is now the second-fastest-growing sport on earth, helping to make Spartan Race worth tens of millions of dollars.

How is this possible? How could Joe defy doctors, defy physical limits, and defy the odds of building a successful company all at the same time? In his words, his success comes from his "frame of reference."

The Frame of Reference

The sun was scorching as Joe pushed himself through the final leg of the Utah Ironman Triathlon. By this point, he had completed twenty Ironmans in his life, but on this day he felt like he had finally met his match. He'd completed the 2.4 miles of swimming and 112 miles of biking, and was 10 miles into the 26.2-mile run to the finish line.

But then Joe's body gave up. He was so nauseous that he had to run to an ambulance on the side of the road, where he started vomiting uncontrollably. The idea of quitting—an idea that had never once popped into his head before—finally seemed logical. After all, what else did he have to prove? He had already completed twenty Ironman triathlons.

He was about to add his name to the "Did Not Finish" list when he saw something out of the corner of his eye. He witnessed a woman with a full prosthetic leg running right by him with a smile on her face. Somehow, this woman had completed the swimming, biking, and ten miles of the running with only one leg—and she still had a smile on her face.

This shifted Joe's frame of reference. No longer was he feeling sorry for himself or wondering what the point was. How could he feel sorry for himself when this woman was taking on a challenge that most two-legged people never attempt? So he summoned the willpower to get out of the ambulance and catch up to her. Then he pushed himself through the heat, through the pain, and through the nausea to keep pace with this woman all the way to the finish line.

What happened here? Clearly, Joe's body had given up. It had already been through the torture of over ten hours of physical exercise in the hot sun and was causing him to vomit uncontrollably. Joe was so sick and in so much pain that even he, who clearly didn't give up easily, was finally about to quit. But all it took was the simple change in perspective provided by the one-legged woman to not only get him back to running, but to motivate him to keep pace with her for sixteen more miles. Facing the heat, the exhaustion, and the nausea, Joe De Sena used his willpower to put one foot in front of the other all the way to the finish line. But what was the source of this willpower?

What Is Willpower?

The students arrived in the laboratory completely starving. Each one of them had been instructed to skip their previous two meals in preparation for this experiment. Then a group of psychologists, led by Roy Baumeister, unleashed their cruelty: They invited the participants into a room filled with the smell of freshly baked chocolate chip cookies.

The aroma was overwhelming as the students, with their stomachs growling, sat down around a table. On the table, there were two plates. One was a plate of the warm, tempting cookies.

The other was a plate of cold, raw radishes. Half of the students were invited to eat as many of the freshly baked cookies as they would like. The unlucky other half of the students were invited to "indulge" in the radishes.

The researchers then left the students alone in the room. The radish-eaters were clearly struggling with the temptation. Some stared longingly at the forbidden treats as if they had not eaten in weeks. Others picked up the cookies and inhaled the aroma. But, as the experiment required, they denied themselves the cookies and stuck to the radishes.

After several minutes of the cookie-eaters rejoicing and the radish-eaters languishing, the students were taken to another room and instructed to work on a geometry puzzle. The students believed that the puzzle was testing their intelligence, but in fact, the puzzle was impossible to solve. The researchers were really testing how long it would be before each student lost the energy to try another strategy to solve the puzzle. This test of perseverance would allow researchers to see just how much willpower each student had.

The cookie-eaters worked on the puzzle for about twenty minutes on average, trying to solve it from multiple angles before finally succumbing to defeat. The radish-eaters, on the other hand, reacted quite differently to the puzzle. They were visibly frustrated, many of them lashing out at the researchers. They told the researchers that the whole experiment was "stupid" and gave up on the puzzle after just eight minutes—less than half the time of the cookie-eaters.

It seemed as if the radish-eaters had used up their willpower to resist the temptation of the cookies, so they had less left to persist on the challenging puzzle. The cookie-eaters, on the other hand, did not have to exert any willpower in the first room, so they had conserved their mental resources for the puzzle.

The Willpower Muscle

This finding shocked researchers. It seemed that we had been looking at the concept of willpower completely wrong. It was not a virtue or a skill, like we had always thought; willpower, it seemed, was actually more like a muscle. When you use it for one exercise, you weaken it for the next.

This explains why getting home from a long day of work can make you feel too exhausted to go to the gym, even if you just sat at a desk all day. It also explains why those who are attempting to quit smoking have a harder time saying "no" to fast food and why creating a huge list of resolutions for the New Year never works.

A professional who is used to sleeping in and grabbing a bagel on the way to work is doomed to fail if she sets a goal to wake up early, resist the morning coffee, force down a healthy breakfast, *and* make it to the gym. She may be able to keep it up for a while, but eventually the alarm will go off and she'll hit the snooze button. A student who is used to partying through the semester and cramming for exams at the last minute is doomed to fail if he resolves to give up drinking and spend his nights in the library. After a week or two, he will be right back to playing beer pong. And an athlete who is used to eating whatever she wants is doomed to fail if she sets a goal to completely cut processed foods out of her diet. It will not be too long before her cravings for salty snacks and sweet desserts become too strong to ignore.

All of those tasks put extraordinary strain on your willpower and leave it too weak to stick with a new routine for the long term. Creating new behaviors isn't easy. You must slowly strengthen your willpower as you add more good behaviors to your lifestyle, just like it takes time and slow progress before you can run a marathon.

But what does it mean to strengthen your willpower? What exactly was happening inside of the brains of the cookie- and radish-eaters?

The Primitive Brain and the Modern Brain

There it is. The piece of cake on the dessert cart that seems all too tempting. Despite your goals of health and fitness, it feels like your entire body is willing you to say, "YES!! Eat the cake!! Get it before the dessert cart leaves!!"

Then another voice comes into the picture. It says, "But wait a minute! This is a new year! And I promised myself that I would resist desserts!"

The internal debate ensues. Sometimes you give in to temptation. Sometimes you summon the willpower to resist. We all face this challenge. The short-term temptation could be unhealthy food, a distraction from work, or staying with friends for another drink. Whatever it is, you face a direct competition between what you *want* to do and what you *should* do.

You know you *should* resist the unhealthy food to become the slimmer, healthier self that you want to be. You know you *should* get your work done now, so you won't be stressed and trying get it done at the last minute. You know you *should* close your tab, head home, get a good night's sleep, and be productive tomorrow morning.

But doing what you *should* is not always easy. Part of you wants to be healthy, be productive, and build for a better future. But another part of you wants to indulge, kick back, and live for the moment. A situation like this is a reflection of two different parts of your brain with competing desires, motivations, and controls over your final decision.

You see, millions of years ago, our ancestors had three very simple goals:

1) Find food.

2) Find a mate.

3) Stay safe from predators.

These three goals were our key to survival, and they were not exactly easy to achieve. Back then, humans were weak and vulnerable creatures. We stood less than five feet tall. We did not have the strength of a gorilla, the talons of an eagle, or the teeth of a tiger. All we had to defend ourselves was our superior intelligence. Over time, this resulted in our brains developing to give us the energy and motivations to meet those top three priorities.

When we saw a chance of getting food, our brains gave us an extraordinary level of energy and focus to help us hunt that food down. When we saw a chance for reproducing, our brains gave us a rush of desire to ensure we did not miss the opportunity. And when we began to exert ourselves too much, our brains gave us the motivation to rest so that we could conserve our energy. These basic motivations were developed in what is called the *limbic system*—or, as I will refer to it throughout this book, the *primitive brain*.

After many years of navigating the wilderness alone, our ancestors came across a novel concept: It is much easier to find food, find a mate, and stay safe from predators if we work together. So we humans started forming tribes. This added a layer of complexity to those three primary goals. Now that we were part of a tribe, we had to learn how to work together. This meant that we not only had to learn to communicate, but we also had to learn to control our actions. Now there were socially acceptable rules we had to abide by, as well:

1) No stealing someone else's food.

2) No stealing someone else's mate.

3) No stealing someone else's shelter.

To abide by these rules, we had to develop a new level of intelligence. We had to learn how to control the basic desires of our primitive brain: to eat as much as we can, sleep with as many people as we can, and stay in the safest possible shelter. If we gave in to those desires, we risked being exiled from the tribe and left to fend for ourselves.

This new level of intelligence was *self-control*. It caused us to think about our higher goal—staying in the tribe—and not let our basic desires compromise it. This led to the development of the *prefrontal cortex*, or as I will refer to it, the *modern brain*.

Even in today's developed society, you are still motivated by these two competing sections of your brain. The primitive brain motivates you to hunt down that cake because it still believes that the cake's fat and sugar will help you survive. The primitive brain also gives you desires to buy things associated with sexual images, because it believes doing so will increase your chances of reproducing. And it will motivate you to conserve your energy, rather than going for a jog.

So it is up to your modern brain to override your primitive brain to accomplish your higher goals. It is your modern brain's job to control your desire for cake so that you can be healthy, the same way it was its job to control your ancestors' desire for others' food so that they could remain in the tribe.

The tension that exists between these two brain segments can make you feel like you have two minds. It is why there will always be an internal debate between your short-term desires and your long-term goals. Your primitive brain still believes that food, sex, and rest are a matter of life and death, so it is up to your modern brain to think about the consequences of those desires and control them. And the fuel your modern brain uses to control your primitive brain is willpower.

Categories of Willpower

If you were to ask ten different people what they use their willpower for, you would get ten different answers. We use it to get out of bed, to eat healthy, to stop procrastinating, to stay up late studying, and to take on hundreds of other challenges. But do all of these activities use the same willpower muscle in the same way?

In her book *The Willpower Instinct,* Stanford health psychologist Kelly McGonigal describes the ways in which we use our willpower by breaking them into three categories: *will power, won't power,* and *want power.*

Will power is the type of willpower the students used to persevere on the puzzle. It is what you use to force yourself out of bed when the alarm goes off, it is what you use to make it to the gym, and it is what you use to stay late working at the office. Anytime your natural inclination is to stop, rest, or give up, but you make the conscious decision to take action instead, you are exerting this form of willpower. When Wolfgang Amadeus Mozart practiced relentlessly on challenging pieces of music, he was using his will power.

Won't power is what most people think about when they think of willpower. It is the ability to say "no" to temptations such as food and shopping sprees. It is what you use to control your emotions and hold your tongue in front of the boss. Anytime your natural desire is to act on an impulse and you make the conscious decision to control your behavior, you are exerting this form of willpower. When Kobe Bryant decided he was going to completely cut sugar out of his diet, he was using his won't power.

Want power is the most important and powerful form of willpower that you have at your disposal. It is the ability to see the higher purpose behind your actions and work toward your long-term goals. Anytime you feel like there is just no way you can ignore a temptation or persevere through a challenge, yet you find something deep within you that enables you to do the right thing, you are exerting this form of willpower. When Joe De Sena found the strength to run with the one-legged woman to the finish line, he was using his want power.

Each category of willpower is exerted in your modern brain, but the categories do not exhaust your willpower muscle in the same way. As you saw in the cookies and radishes experiment, will power and won't power use the same energy source. The radish-eaters used their won't power to resist the cookies, so they had less will power to persevere on the puzzle. Want power, however, acts much differently. Although it still requires energy to use your want power, it requires much less energy than do will power and won't power. When you are fully committed to a passion, purpose, or long-term goal—so committed that you tap into your want power—you will use less mental energy and have more endurance than if you were to use your will power or won't power alone.

For example, take two men who are successful executives. One man is happily married, and the other is single. Both men begin receiving sexual advances from an attractive young coworker. Both men also know that having sex with a coworker is a bad idea. The happily married man, however, will have a much easier time saying no to the temptation because he has a commitment to a greater purpose—his marriage, his family, his love—than will the single man who does not have the same commitment. The married man will use his want power to resist the temptation because the prospect of sex is not nearly as valuable to him as his family, whereas the single man will have to use his won't power, making it harder for him to resist the temptation.

This same phenomenon occurs in many other challenges as well. A father will have an easier time quitting drinking if he does it to be a good role model for his children. An athlete will push herself harder if she is training for a marathon than if she is just jogging for recreation. An employee who derives a sense of purpose from her daily work will find it easier to get out of bed in the morning than if she was doing a menial job. In all of these cases, people are still exerting their willpower, but it is far less taxing for them than it would be if they were doing so without a higher purpose.

You will find the journey to your goals much easier if you use your want power as much as possible—and tapping into it is much simpler than you may think. You do not need to have an inspiring purpose, a meaningful job, or even a one-legged woman run by you in order to shift to your want power. A simple change in perspective is all it takes.

Changing Your Perspective

When you make a plan to accomplish your goals, you probably begin by setting up steps that you "have to" follow. You want to become more fit, so you *have to* go to the gym three times per week. When your friends invite you out after work, you politely decline, claiming that you *have to* go to the gym. All the while, your brain is paying attention to these cues. When you say that you "have to" do something, you are sending your brain a message that there are other things that you want to do, but you're restricted by a plan that you set days, weeks, or months ago. When you view this plan as an obligation that you *have to* follow, your primitive brain will begin to motivate you to stop following it—especially when you are low on willpower. Your primitive brain wants you to take the easy way out, so it will come up with excuses for you to take a break today and resume your plan tomorrow.

You can turn this primitive instinct off, however, by changing your message from "have to" to "get to." You *get to* go to the gym today and improve your fitness. You *get to* order a salad for lunch instead of pizza, and feel good about yourself afterward. You *get to* engage in deliberate practice to become great in your field. This simple technique will shift your brain from using will power to using the more effective want power.

Similarly, when most people take up the popular practice of watching their weight, their typical response to a temptation is to say, "I can't." But—as with "have to"—is it possible that saying "I can't" might actually *increase* the likelihood that these people will give in? Researchers at Boston College wanted to find out, so they brought a group of undergraduate students into the lab to test if *how* you say "no" to a temptation matters.

They separated the students into two groups. Both groups were dieters with the intention of cutting out sweets. They were both offered Hershey's Kisses and asked to resist the temptation to eat them for twenty-four hours. One group was given the instruction to resist by saying, "I can't eat chocolate," and the other was given the instruction to say, "I don't eat chocolate." Then they were to bring back the same Hershey's Kisses the next day to prove that they had resisted the temptation (the researchers marked the Kisses to ensure that nobody cheated by bringing in different ones). The next day, only 39 percent of those who said "I can't eat chocolate" were able to resist the temptation. Meanwhile, 62 percent of those who said "I don't eat chocolate" were able stay strong. Simply saying "I don't" instead of "I can't" made the dieters almost twice as effective in resisting temptation.

As with "get to" and "have to," saying "I don't" rather than "I can't" shifts your perspective. Think about what you're really saying when you use "I can't." You're saying that you *would* eat the chocolate, but there is some outside reason that is preventing you from indulging. It doesn't matter if that outside reason is an experiment or a diet plan; you see it as some factor that is preventing you from having what you really want. "I don't," however, changes your perspective to that of a person making a conscious choice to not eat chocolate. You begin to identify yourself as someone who *chooses* to eat healthy. This will shift you from won't power to want power, and your cravings for your vices will begin to subside as a result.

The Power of Perspective

Three hundred and fifty miles of pain and suffering: that's what Joe De Sena and his three teammates were looking at as they approached the starting line of the 2001 International Raid Ukatak. The Raid Ukatak is an adventure race held in Quebec, Canada, in the middle of the winter. Yet Joe's team was ready and willing to endure torture.

This was Joe's first real test of his willpower. He was not much of an athlete at that point, especially compared to his teammates, who all had decades of experience. In order to make it through the race, he would have to rely on his mental strength much more than his physical strength.

The race began with him and his team iceboating down the Saint Lawrence River. It was so cold that they may as well have been in the Arctic. Floating ice would constantly knock into their boat, sending the team overboard and into the freezing river. Without any dry clothes, they had to simply endure the pain of being wet and frozen. And this was just the beginning of the six-day race.

After the Saint Lawrence, they hiked for two days in snow that was knee-deep. This was so tiring that Joe needed to chug a bottle of olive oil in order to keep going. He had to ignore every human impulse to stop and rest. He had to silence the shouting of his primitive brain in order to keep putting one foot in front of the other.

Then he started to literally lose his mind. He saw members of his family, he saw fast food restaurants, and he smelled the delicious aroma of a cheeseburger—and he wasn't even halfway to the finish line. So how did he and his team not only persevere through the next 150-plus miles of the race, but also become one of the first teams to cross the finish line?

Joe thought about an explorer named Ernest Shackleton. In 1912, Shackleton led an expedition of fifty-six men to be the first to cross Antarctica. From the very beginning, the expedition was doomed. Shackleton's ship crashed into ice hundreds of miles from the shores of Antarctica. He and his crew spent over a year trying to get home, traveling over 1,000 miles in temperatures much colder than those in Canada, in a place where nobody could help them. Compared to that situation, the journey to the end of the race didn't seem so bad.

How you view a situation matters. If you see working toward your goal as an opportunity, rather than an obligation, you are going to use less willpower and enjoy it more. If you see yourself as a healthy, fit, or organized person, it will be easier to act like that person. And if you confront your challenges with the proper perspective, and understand that it really isn't so bad, then you will gain confidence to overcome them, just like Joe De Sena did.

Conclusion

Willpower is not a metaphor. There is a real science behind the mental strength that it takes to pull yourself out of bed in the morning, deny yourself tempting foods, and push your body sixteen more miles after it has said "enough." The biggest mistake that people make with their willpower is putting far too many demands on it. When you use willpower to persevere through a long, stressful day of work, you're not going to have as much left to lace up your running shoes or cook yourself a healthy dinner.

But even when your willpower is at its weakest, you can still stick to your goals by shifting your perspective and engaging your want power. You will have more willpower to commit to deliberate practice if you "get to" do it, rather than "have to" do it. Similarly, you will have more willpower to deny temptations if you "don't" indulge, rather than "can't" indulge. Understanding these principles is the first step toward using your willpower to achieve greatness.

Key Points

- *Willpower is a muscle.* Willpower is not a talent, a skill, or even a virtue. It actually works just like a muscle. That's why you can feel exhausted after a long day of work, even if you just sat at a desk all day.

- *Your short-term desires come from your primitive brain.* Your cravings for food and relaxation come from a primitive part of your brain that was developed long ago. This part of your brain is a powerful motivator, but it doesn't call the shots.

- *Your long-term desires come from your modern brain.* Your desires for long-term accomplishments come from a more modernly developed part of your brain. This is where your willpower resides, and it has the ultimate say over your actions.

- *There are three types of willpower: will power, won't power, and want power.* Will power is the ability to work toward your goal. Won't power is the ability to resist temptations. Want power is the ability to believe in the larger purpose and do whatever it takes.

- *You perspective can make a big difference.* How you view a situation matters. If you see your work toward your goal as an opportunity, not an obligation, it will require less willpower to achieve it.

Strategies

1) *Set as few goals as possible.* Science suggests setting no more than three goals at a time to avoid overloading your willpower muscle.

2) *Say "get to" instead of "have to."* This will shift your brain from will power to want power.

3) *Say "I don't" instead of "I can't."* This will shift your brain from won't power to want power.

4) *Reframe your perspective.* When you think there is no way you can reach your goal, reframe your perspective, as Joe De Sena did with the one-legged triathlete.

Chapter 3

Fueling Your Willpower

"Understand what you're putting into your body. What you put in is as important as what you take out."
– Tim Grover

His heart was racing, his hands were sweaty, and he knew this was going to be his one chance to impress the great Michael Jordan. He was not going to let this opportunity slip by. Tim Grover always knew he was going to train world-class athletes, and now he was getting the chance to meet personally with one of the greatest basketball players in the world. Grover had been calling the Chicago Bulls for a meeting every day since he learned that Michael was looking to improve his strength. Michael didn't want to be pushed around by the Detroit Pistons anymore, and he was willing to do whatever it took to make sure of that. So Grover created a detailed plan that outlined what exercises Michael would do, how much sleep he would get, and which food he would eat.

After the Bulls management had one meeting with Grover, they arranged for him to pitch to Michael in person. Grover explained his plan down to the finest detail, and Michael was not convinced. But Grover would not be denied. He talked for another hour about the benefits of his program, until Michael finally relented and decided to try it for thirty days. He ended up following it for the next fifteen years.

The training and diet regimen that Grover put Michael through was so intense that when Michael finally retired, he told Grover, "If I ever see you in my neighborhood again, I'm going to shoot you."

Since that time, Tim Grover has worked with top-notch basketball players from all over the world. The list includes Charles Barkley, Hakeem Olajuwon, Kobe Bryant, and Dwyane Wade. His training methods are so intense that even superstar athletes are seen vomiting into trash cans within the first thirty minutes of the program.

When someone starts vomiting, it doesn't matter how physically fit he may be, he needs extraordinary willpower in order to continue exercising. Yet somehow Grover's athletes are able to develop the mental strength to endure this rigorous training. This might be due to Grover's screams of "encouragement," but more likely it is due to the three sources of fuel he gives his athletes: food, sleep, and exercise.

The Breakfast of Champions

"I can't lose weight. I'm thirty pounds over where I need to be," one of Grover's athletes told him as he was preparing for the season. "I don't get it. I'm working out every day, no drinking. Eating healthy..."

"Tell me what you're eating," Grover demanded.

"Oh, you know, healthy. I start my day with a huge smoothie..."

"What's in the smoothie?"

"Healthy stuff. Orange juice, pineapple, strawberries, bananas, blueberries, granola, yogurt...very healthy."

"Got it. Good news: If you're consuming that much sugar every morning, be grateful you're only thirty pounds overweight. It could be a lot worse, and probably will be, because there are more sugars in that smoothie than the average person should consume in an entire day."

What does Grover mean by this? Well, sugar is what the body will burn through first when it begins exerting energy. So rather than burning any of the thirty pounds of fat that that athlete had, his body was instead just burning through his morning smoothie. That left his body with just as much fat at the end of the workout as it had at the beginning—no matter how difficult that workout was. So what does Grover have his athletes eat instead of this "healthy" food that is actually full of sugar?

"I give my athletes what I call 'The List': a yes/no inventory of foods they can eat and those they can't. Here are your options, here's what you're giving up. No sugar, no dairy, no fruit, no breads, no alcohol. No junk."

The foods that Grover forbids his athletes from eating are high-glycemic foods, so called because they lead to a sharp increase in blood sugar. Grover only allows his athletes to eat low-glycemic foods, those that increase blood sugar gradually. These foods include eggs, meat, vegetables, nuts, and other low-carbohydrate foods.

On this diet, Grover's athletes burn through the extra fat they have on them and not just the sugar they ate for breakfast. This helps them get into better shape every day as they progress through Grover's program. And, whether Grover realizes it or not, his athletes' bodies aren't the only thing affected by this diet. The diet also affects their willpower.

The Effects of Sugar on Willpower

The students arrived at the high school having skipped the most important meal of the day: breakfast. Upon their arrival, each student was separated into one of three groups. The first group received a healthy breakfast of low-glycemic foods such as eggs and oatmeal; the second group received an unhealthy breakfast of high-glycemic foods such as bagels, muffins, and pastries; and the final group received no breakfast at all.

The teachers, who were not aware of which students were in which group, were instructed to rate each student on his or her behavior and academic performance during the morning periods, from eight o'clock to ten thirty. At ten thirty, students from all three groups would be given the same low-glycemic snack, after which the teachers would again grade each of the students on the same measures of behavior and academic performance, from ten thirty until one o'clock in the afternoon.

This study was originally designed to understand the effects of breakfast on academic performance and behavior. We all want to set our kids up for success in school, so we need to know what difference, if any, breakfast has on their academic performance. What the researchers found, however, was much more important than the simple cliché of breakfast as "the most important meal of the day."

Across the board, students with the low-glycemic breakfast greatly outperformed the others on the measures of behavior and academics in the early time slot. The students who ate the high-glycemic breakfast were graded well at the beginning, but as it got closer to ten thirty, they started to act out and lose their focus. The students who ate no breakfast at all performed the worst on both measures. They were undisciplined, unmotivated, and inattentive throughout the morning periods. These ratings were consistent regardless of each student's academic history, family situation, or school citations. "Bad kids" who ate the healthy breakfast still performed better on both measures than the "good kids" who ate the unhealthy breakfast or went without one at all.

This may not come as much of a shock to you; after all, this proves what we have been told for years: Breakfast really is important! The truly interesting finding, however, comes from the second time period, after each student ate a low-glycemic snack. After the snack, all of the differences in behavior and performance between the three groups vanished. The students who were acting out in the morning suddenly found the ability to listen to their teachers, do their assigned work, and receive the same marks as those students who had eaten the low-glycemic breakfast. It was almost as if all of the students were given a dose of self-control to improve their behavior, focus on their work, and increase their ability to think critically.

As with Grover's athletes, low-glycemic foods seemed to perform miracles on the students' performances. But what exactly is it about low-glycemic foods that increases the willpower of both high school students in the classroom and professional athletes on the basketball court?

The Willpower Fuel

Determining what might fuel willpower is not easy. After all, think about everything people consume to increase mental energy. People use coffee, Red Bull, Gatorade, soda, and many other performance beverages. Then there are celebrations like New Year's Eve and Mardi Gras, where people use a night of indulgence to prepare for an extended period of virtue. Any of these methods could fuel willpower in some way. But after several experiments, psychologist Matthew Gailliot and his team finally found a conclusive answer.

The group of researchers invited hungry students into a laboratory and separated them into three groups. The first group received a chocolaty, creamy, old-fashioned milk shake. The second group received a tasteless milk-based product with the exact same number of calories and nutrients as the milk shake. The third group did not receive anything.

After indulging in their respective drinks, the students were then asked to do a set of self-control tasks, like the unsolvable puzzle from the cookie and radish experiment. The point of the study was to determine if indulging in the tasty milk shake would help the students persevere longer on self-control tasks than drinking the tasteless one (or nothing at all). It made sense in theory; after all, the cookie-eaters had lasted longer than the radish-eaters.

But the results told a different story. The students from both the chocolate and the tasteless milk shake groups performed the same on the self-control tasks, while the control group who did not receive anything lagged behind. Clearly, these students' self-control was being fueled by something other than indulgence. It turned out that it was not merely indulging that fueled their willpower; it was the nutrients they received from the milkshake.

Specifically, it was the chemical *glucose*. Glucose is the human body's key source of energy. It is absorbed from the food that we eat and transported throughout the body via the bloodstream. The brain, which uses about 20 percent of the body's energy, relies on glucose to do everything from regulating bodily functions, to learning new languages, to—yes—exerting willpower.

Because both drinks had the same nutrients, the bodies of both groups of students produced the same amount of glucose, leading them to perform similarly on their tests of self-control. This also explains why both groups of students who drank milk shakes outperformed those who did not drink anything. Since the control group did not have any extra glucose in their systems, their brains didn't have any fuel for their willpower. This finding led to the next question on researchers' minds: Which foods supply you with the most willpower fuel?

Good Glucose and Bad Glucose

Any food that contains calories will give your brain glucose to work with, but not all glucose is created equally. High-glycemic foods like donuts, muffins, candy, and soda will cause a quick spike of glucose—giving you willpower fuel for the short term—but will then cause a subsequent crash that immediately depletes your willpower. This is why the students who ate the unhealthy breakfast of bagels, muffins, and pastries performed well at the beginning but lost discipline as time passed. They had a short-term spike of willpower that was not sustainable.

To get the most willpower fuel, you should follow a diet similar to the one Tim Grover designs for his athletes. It is full of food that provides the brain with long-term willpower fuel and completely devoid of food that creates the spike-and-crash effect. That is why his athletes have the ability to keep pushing through an intense workout. They may "hit a wall" physically during one of their training sessions, but their willpower will remain steady thanks to their bodies' consistent supply of glucose to the brain.

If you can cut high-glycemic food of any kind out of your diet, your brain will be loaded with long-term willpower. And even if Grover's diet seems a little bit too strict to you, don't worry (unless you're a professional basketball player). Any of the foods listed below are great low-glycemic options that will give you long-term willpower:

- *Lean proteins.* This includes cuts of beef, poultry, pork, fish, and free-range eggs.

- *Nuts.* Those nuts that are high in omega-3 fatty acids, like walnuts, pecans, and cashews, are particularly beneficial.

- *Vegetables.* All vegetables will help build your long-term willpower, so the best strategy is to choose vegetables that you are willing to eat consistently.

- *Fresh fruit.* Yes, Grover doesn't allow fruit in his diet, but many fruits like berries and avocados are actually low-glycemic foods.

If you can't remember this list at all times, just remember this general rule: You will get much more long-term willpower out of food that looks like, well, food. The closer the food on your plate looks to the way you would find it in nature, the better. This is because processed foods usually contain high-fructose corn syrup. Any foods that contain high-fructose corn syrup—even those that may be labeled "healthy"—will result in the willpower spike-and-crash effect.

It might be the case that your mouth did not water as you looked over this list of high-willpower foods. In fact, you might even be wondering how you'll be able to summon the willpower to eat these foods. In today's society—where sweet, fattening, and processed food is all around us—it's not easy to eat more lean meats, fruits, vegetables, and non-processed foods in general.

So how can you summon the willpower necessary to eat these healthy foods? And, perhaps more importantly, how can you *avoid* those other foods that will lead to the spike-and-crash effect? To answer these questions, let's look at *why* we crave these tempting foods more than we do broccoli or baked chicken.

Why We Get Cravings

We have done it! thought James Olds, *We have found the happiness center of the brain!*

The year was 1953. James Olds and fellow psychologist Peter Milner had been stimulating various areas of rats' brains to determine how that would affect their behavior. One day, they stimulated an area of the midbrain that they believed was connected to happiness. Whenever they triggered it, the rats seemed to be in a state of complete euphoria.

Even more convincing, they witnessed the remarkable things the rats were willing to do to get another hit of stimulation. They would go wherever the researchers wanted—even over electrocuted floors that burned them—to get their happiness centers stimulated. Naturally, Olds and Milner assumed the rats were doing this because the hit was so pleasurable that it was worth the pain to get it.

After several tests with rats, Olds and Milner turned to humans to see if they could be given the same blissful feeling. If so, that could be vitally important for the treatment of mental illnesses like depression.

Sure enough, the humans acted in the same way. Olds and Milner set people up with the ability to stimulate the happiness area of their brains by simply pressing a button. Subjects then hit the button over and over again, until the researchers had to physically stop them from continuing. It appeared as if these people had reached an extreme level of euphoria.

However, when they asked the subjects what they felt from the shock, they reported that it was not euphoria at all. The shock was actually frustrating them! It turned out that each shock had not produced happiness, but rather the *promise* of happiness.

Olds and Milner had not discovered the area of the brain connected to happiness, but instead the area connected to desire. The brains of these subjects kept saying, "Press that button, and you will be happy!" But the actual happiness never came.

This area of the brain is the same one that is stimulated when you see the dessert tray wheeled by, when you roll the dice in craps, or when your favorite store has a sale. It is telling you, "Get this, and you will be happy!" It is our craving center. But why would our brains give us this promise of happiness? Once again, we must look to our ancestors for the answer.

Back in ancient times, food was scarce. Most of the time, our ancestors were starving and weak. So if they were lucky enough to see clues that a gazelle might be nearby, their brains wanted to give them as much energy and focus to hunt it down as possible. So they started producing a chemical called *dopamine*.

Dopamine activated the reward center of the brain, making our ancestors believe that a gazelle was the most desirable thing in the world. It filled them with a rush of energy, to hunt the gazelle down at all costs while also tuning out any distractions. This gave people the focus, energy, and drive to ignore their feelings of exhaustion and hunt that gazelle down—and as a result, to survive.

Their brains told them to "eat that gazelle, and you will be happy" to help ensure that our species lived on. But once our ancestors ate that gazelle, they would never *actually* be happy, because the next day their brains needed to give them that same desire to hunt down the next gazelle. If they were satisfied or fulfilled by eating just one gazelle, then they would not have been able to gain that same focus and motivation to hunt the next time, and humans would have died out.

Back in today's society—where desires are all around us—our brains function the same way. So we continue to eat, to gamble, and to shop for things that we believe will bring us happiness when, in reality, we will never be satisfied. That primitive survival mechanism will always drive us to seek out that next hit we believe will finally bring us the happiness we desire.

How to Resist Cravings

Now that you know *why* you get a craving, you have already won half the battle in resisting it. You now know that the happiness your brain is promising will not actually be there, because it can't be. But, of course, having this knowledge does not mean that saying "no" to a craving will be easy. So let's go over some strategies that you can use to overcome your primitive instincts and fight back against a craving:

1) *Pause and take five deep breaths.* If you catch yourself thinking that something tempting will make you happy, pause. As you slowly take five deep breaths, think about what is happening in your brain and how it is trying to motivate you. By taking this moment for self-awareness, you will activate the part of your modern brain that is in charge of impulse control. You will remember that the desire you feel will not actually lead to

happiness and will negatively affect your long-term goals. You will switch from using your won't power to using your want power to resist the craving, enabling you to make the right decision. While this technique may seem simple, it is also incredibly effective in helping you push through those heated moments of a craving.

2) *Positive procrastination.* If that first strategy does not work and you still feel like you must give in to your craving, try a tactic known as *positive procrastination.* Your brain believes that it needs to act quickly in order to get a reward—you need to think fast in order to catch a gazelle! But in this day and age, the decision of whether to give in to a craving is probably not a life-and-death choice. So the next time you are staring temptation in the face, put the decision off for just ten minutes. Those ten minutes will calm your reward center down and allow you to make a more rational choice. Then, even if you decide to give in, you can take solace in the fact that you had an extra ten minutes to savor the prospect. In all likelihood, however, you will notice that you do not need that reward as badly as you first thought.

3) *Do not feel guilty.* If both of the above tactics do not work and you give in to the craving, do not feel guilty. Feeling guilty is the natural response to indulging in a craving, but it will only make things worse. You will not be able to fully enjoy the thing that you craved, and the feeling of guilt will also drain your willpower—which means that even though you gave in to the craving, you will use up just as much willpower as if you had exercised your won't power to resist it.

When it comes to cravings, self-control is much easier when you remember that your brain is not wired for the modern world. Instead, it is programmed to help you meet the most basic needs for your survival. That reward center has played a big part in the survival of our species, as we once needed its extra motivation to make up for our lack of strength and energy.

But in today's society, you have the ability to dream of higher aspirations than merely eating, resting, and having sex. So the next time your brain tempts you with a promise of happiness, recognize why it's doing so, take a break, and remember your higher goals.

Back to Breakfast

So what's the best long-term strategy for ensuring that you have a fully stocked reservoir of willpower fuel? The answer is still having a healthy breakfast. What we have been told all of our lives about the importance of breakfast is absolutely true; however, it is not about simply eating a breakfast. It is about eating a *healthy* breakfast that will give you three huge willpower advantages:

- *It will give you a consistent stream of willpower.* If you were to eat a dinner full of low-glycemic foods, you would only see the willpower advantages for the few hours before you went to bed. But if you eat a healthy breakfast, you will have a solid reservoir of willpower fuel for the entire day's worth of self-control challenges.

  This will also increase the likelihood that you will eat healthier at other mealtimes. With the increased level of glucose in your system, you will have more willpower to resist the donuts at the office and more willpower to order the healthiest item on the lunch menu. By eating a healthy breakfast, you are setting yourself up for a healthy snack, healthy lunch, and healthy dinner as well.

- *Your willpower is strongest in the morning.* We all know how hard it can be to work up the willpower to cook yourself a healthy dinner when you are just coming back from a long, stressful day at work. So instead of planning to eat healthy in that moment when your willpower is at its weakest, plan on eating healthy when it is at its strongest. It is much easier to motivate yourself to cook a healthy breakfast in the morning when you have not had to deal with the stresses of the day.

- *It is a small win.* A small win is an extremely important phenomenon in the development of a new behavior. If you are able to summon the willpower to eat a healthy breakfast, you will gain the confidence that you can be a healthy person in other ways. This will make you feel more in control of what you eat for lunch and dinner as well. Starting the day with a small win sets you up for more success throughout the day.

Sleep

What you eat has a strong impact on your willpower, but Tim Grover knew that food alone wasn't enough to get his athletes to peak performance. That's why in addition to setting what they needed to eat, he also set how much they needed to sleep.

Have you ever seen somebody try to exercise his or her willpower after losing sleep? Think of college students during finals week, parents who have been up all night with an infant, and exhausted accountants near the end of tax season—none of them seem to have any self-control. This is no coincidence.

When you do not get enough sleep, your modern brain takes the biggest hit. When you are tired, your brain cells are not able to absorb glucose as efficiently as when you are well rested. This means that you begin losing the power of your willpower.

Your brain will recognize the fact that it is not getting enough glucose and immediately start to crave sugar, fat, and caffeine to replenish its supply. And because your brain cells are not absorbing glucose as efficiently as they should be, not only will you give in to eating that sugar, fat, and caffeine, but you will also consume much more of it than you need. Your brain will continue to crave junk food until it gets as much glucose as it can into your bloodstream—regardless of how many calories that may be. So as you start to lose sleep, you will start to gain weight.

Those extra pounds, however, may not sound so bad when you compare them with another side effect of too little sleep. In addition to weight gain, sleep deprivation also leads to what is called *mild prefrontal dysfunction*, a state in which your brain is unable to regulate your emotions or attention as well as when you have enough sleep. Essentially, this state of mind is like being drunk. You begin to lose your focus, you become irritated by small things, and you can make questionable decisions—a recipe for disaster where willpower is concerned.

College students, new parents, and accountants, of course, are not the only ones who deal with being sleep-deprived. According to the Centers for Disease Control and Prevention (CDC), approximately 38 percent of people were so sleep-deprived that they unintentionally fell asleep during the day at least once in the last month. This, and other similarly shocking statistics, has led the CDC to label sleep deprivation as a national epidemic.

So how do you reverse this trend, take care of your mind, and increase your willpower? The obvious answer to this question is to get more sleep. But for most of us, it is not that simple. We all have many pulls on our time. Sometimes we cannot simply add more hours of sleep to our already-busy schedules. Luckily, there are scientifically proven tactics that will help you get a better night's sleep without adding more hours:

1) *Meditation.* We'll discuss meditation more in the next chapter, but for now, know that adding a daily routine of meditation to your schedule will help revitalize your body and mind to reverse some of the effects of sleep deprivation. Research shows that

just ten minutes of meditation when you are sleep-deprived will have significant benefits on your modern brain's ability to function properly—keeping you out of that "drunken" state of mind and keeping your willpower intact.

2) *A completely dark room.* Most of us underestimate the effect that lights have on our sleep. When your room is completely dark, it helps your brain shut down and sleep more efficiently. This helps you get more rest out of the hours you spend in bed, helping to restore your willpower.

3) *Naps.* Some research suggests that it is the amount of consecutive hours you spend awake that matters the most when it comes to willpower (the more hours, the less willpower), so breaking up the day with a nap can have significant benefits. It is better for your brain to sleep for seven hours at night with a one-hour nap during the day than it is to sleep for eight consecutive hours at night without taking that break.

4) *Building a reservoir.* Although this is not a fail-safe strategy, catching up on sleep has been shown to reverse some effects of sleep deprivation. Getting more sleep on the weekend will create a reserve of energy your brain can use for willpower during the week. So if you cannot squeeze more hours of sleep in during the week, see if you can catch up on the weekend.

The importance of a good night's sleep has been proven again and again by experts all over the world. If you find it challenging to resist temptations or maintain your focus, it could be that your lack of sleep is setting you up for failure. Many people blame themselves for not having enough willpower, when really they should be blaming their sleep schedules. If you cannot find the time to add more sleep into your daily routine, try meditating, making your room completely dark, napping, or building a reservoir of sleep on the weekends. Although these are not perfect replacements for more sleep, they have been proven to improve your brain's ability to process glucose. This will help enormously in fueling your willpower.

Exercise

Two of the key advantages that Grover's athletes have with their willpower is that they eat well and that they get good sleep. But what about the act of exercise itself? Is it possible that regular exercise can affect your willpower too?

That was the question Megan Oaten and Ken Cheng at Macquarie University in Sydney were trying to answer. There are, of course, many physical health benefits associated with exercise: lower cholesterol, less risk of heart disease, lower chance of obesity, and increase in physical energy. But is it possible that exercise could benefit our mental health as well?

To find out, Oaten and Cheng selected twenty-four non-exercisers between the ages of eighteen and fifty to participate in a two-month study. They were given free gym memberships and asked to exercise just once per week for the first month and then increase to three times per week for the second month. Then, throughout the course of the study, the researchers tested the participants on various self-control activities, from resisting temptations to persevering through challenging tasks.

The results were nothing short of remarkable. After just two months of exercise, every participant had indeed increased his or her ability to resist temptations and persevere on challenging tasks—and the benefits did not end there! The participants also:

- Procrastinated less;

- Felt more in control of their emotions;

- Reduced their nicotine/tobacco, alcohol, and caffeine intake;

- Saved more money;

- Ate less junk food;

- Watched less television;

- Spent more time studying;

- Splurged less on impulse purchases; and

- Were more likely to be on time to appointments.

All of these positive changes occurred naturally as a result of habitual exercise.

The best part of the study's findings was just how little exercise was required in order to achieve these benefits. It is important to remember that for a full month, these participants only went to the gym *once per week*. That means they only went four times total in the entire first month.

When trying to establish your own exercise plan, it is clearly not necessary for you to get carried away. To start getting all of the benefits listed above, you just need to make a plan that is consistent. Whether you can exercise once per week or four times per week does not matter all that much. When it comes to your willpower, the important thing is to be consistent. Set a plan that you know you will be able to execute with uncompromising consistency. Consistency is the key to getting the remarkable results attained by these participants.

The next piece of good news about exercise is that, according to Kelly McGonigal, you can pick and choose what type you would like to do. Although there are many different physical benefits based on the type of exercise you choose, the brain has no preference. You will get roughly the same willpower benefits whether you choose to go for a jog or do push-ups. As long as you are doing *something*, you will see the willpower benefits of exercise.

Regular physical exercise is one of the best techniques you can use to boost your willpower. Unfortunately, many people never get to see the full benefits of exercise because they set unrealistic workout schedules and are not able to remain consistent. When coming up with a plan to exercise, remember that consistency is far more important than frequency. It does not matter if you start by lifting weights or by going for a walk. As long as you remain consistent, you will build up your willpower muscle and become strong both physically and mentally.

Conclusion

Tim Grover has trained some of the greatest basketball players of our time. Part of the reason for their success is because they trained at such a high intensity that even the best among them could not last thirty minutes without vomiting. To make it through a workout like that, you don't just need phenomenal physical strength—you need phenomenal mental strength.

Whether he knew it or not, Grover's diet, sleep, and exercise plan helped his athletes survive his workouts because they had a consistent supply of willpower fuel. You can achieve the same long-term willpower benefit for yourself by sticking to low-glycemic foods, sleeping better, and getting some exercise. You don't even need to completely overhaul your life; just ensure that you always start your day with a low-glycemic breakfast, that you get as much quality sleep as you can, and that you exercise consistently. You'll be amazed at how that feeds your willpower through the whole day.

Key Points

- *Your brain uses glucose to fuel your willpower.* Like other muscles in your body, your willpower requires fuel. That fuel is glucose, which your body gathers from the food you eat.

- *Low-glycemic foods are the most effective for fueling your willpower.* Lean protein, vegetables, nuts, fruit, and other non-processed foods are the most effective at fueling your willpower.

- *Cravings come from the primitive brain.* Cravings for unhealthy food come from the primitive brain's survival instincts. Although they still have the power to motivate, your modern brain has control over them.

- *Sleep refuels your willpower.* Sleep helps to restore the glucose your brain uses to exert willpower while also helping it exert willpower more efficiently. If you can't get more sleep at night, you can still try to make the sleep you do get more effective.

- *Exercise increases your willpower efficiency.* Regular physical exercise will help your brain process glucose more efficiently. It does not matter what type of exercise you do, as long as it's an activity you're willing to do consistently.

Strategies

1) *Eat a low-glycemic breakfast.* A healthy low-glycemic breakfast will give you a consistent stream of willpower to use throughout the day.

2) *Pause and plan.* If you have a craving, take a minute to pause, take five deep breaths, and understand that you have control over the situation.

3) *Positive procrastination.* If you still have a craving, put the decision to indulge off for just ten minutes. You will often find that, by then, the craving has disappeared.

4) *Do not feel guilty.* If you do end up indulging, do not feel guilty. It will only decrease your willpower and make you even more likely to give in next time.

5) *Get the most willpower out of your sleep.* If you can't add more hours of sleep, try meditating, making your room completely dark, having a nap, or building a sleep reservoir on the weekend.

6) *Choose a fun, consistent exercise routine.* You will get the same willpower benefits whether you're lifting weights or playing volleyball. And whatever you choose, do not go overboard. Once per week for six months is better than six times for one week and never going again.

Chapter 4

Strengthening Your Willpower

"Magic is pretty simple: It comes down to training, practice, and experimentation, followed up by ridiculous pursuit and relentless perseverance."
– David Blaine

David Blaine didn't know how much longer he could last. He had been encased in a block of ice in the middle of Times Square for a full fifty-five hours and was literally going crazy.

"I started to think I was in purgatory. I genuinely believed I was being judged, and that this was a place I was waiting to go to heaven or hell," Blaine later said of his experience in Roy Baumeister and John Tierny's book *Willpower: Rediscovering the Greatest Human Strength*.

As soon as he'd stepped inside of the block of ice those many hours ago, he'd immediately started shivering. After the twenty-four-hour mark, he began fighting sleep deprivation. He couldn't sit down or fall asleep because doing so would expose his bare skin to the ice and result in frostbite. So he had been willing himself to keep upright and fighting the urge to nod off for thirty-nine hours.

Then it got even worse. The unseasonably warm weather in New York caused some of the ice to melt, which led a steady drip of cold water to trickle down Blaine's neck. He was enduring torture.

Now, at the fifty-five-hour mark, the sleep deprivation was so bad that Blaine was hallucinating. He heard voices, he saw bodies carved into the ice, and he even saw his own judgment day, hoping that he had lived a good enough life to be sent to heaven.

"Those last eight hours were the worst state I've ever been in. To go through something that horrific and not quit—that took something that was beyond me."

Yet he *did* make it through those last eight hours. Somehow, David Blaine endured the cold, the dripping ice water, the sleep deprivation, and the mental illness for an entire working day. But how did he do it?

Many simply do not believe it was possible. After all, David Blaine is a magician. It could have all been illusion, the same way it was with Blaine's hero Harry Houdini. But perhaps those people might not be so skeptical if they knew about the mental training exercises Blaine has been doing since he was a young boy.

The Strength of Willpower

When David Blaine was four years old, he got his first exposure to magic. He saw a magician in the subway near his home in Brooklyn perform the Pencil Through Card trick, and Blaine was completely blown away. He couldn't believe the man had been able to do that! But unlike other children who were simply awestruck by magic, Blaine was determined to learn it. Like the young Mozart, Blaine became obsessed.

Unfortunately, his family could not afford to buy him anything from a magic shop, so he used tarot cards that his grandmother gave him to practice with. In addition to practicing with the cards, he also spent countless hours at the library reading everything he could about magic.

When Blaine turned five, he showed a neighbor a magic trick he had created with the tarot cards. The man was in awe, unable to believe that this kid had performed a magic trick that he couldn't figure out. The neighbor's response showed Blaine the amazing effect that magic can have on people. He knew then that he wanted to become a showman. And, like Leopold Mozart,

Blaine's mother supported her son's dream in every way she could. But little did she know that magic would not be enough. Blaine didn't just want to perform unbelievable feats of magic; he wanted to perform unbelievable feats of will.

As Baumeister and Tierney describe, aside from enduring hours of deliberate practice with his magic tricks, the young Blaine also engaged in deliberate practice with his willpower. He would swim for as long as possible without coming up for air. He would walk to school in the dead of winter in only a T-shirt. He would run barefoot in the snow for as long as he could. He would take freezing-cold baths to see how long he could stay in the water. He even spent three whole days in a closet without moving.

When he turned eleven, he fasted for four days without anything but water. Then he more than doubled that feat when he turned eighteen and fasted for ten days with only water and wine. Just like Wolfgang Amadeus Mozart, Kobe Bryant, and the other heroes in this book, David Blaine also had to endure 10,000 hours of deliberate practice in order to achieve greatness in his field. But his skill wasn't music, sports, or business—it was willpower itself.

Willpower Practice

David Blaine is proof that willpower really is like a muscle. Not only does it get tired from overuse and fueled by the right diet, but it can also be strengthened with practice. However, my guess is that you do not have any desire to plop into a bath of freezing-cold water or trap yourself in a closet for three days. So what are some ways that you can strengthen your willpower without enduring the bizarre torture that Blaine put himself through?

To answer this question, psychologist Mark Muraven—with guidance from Roy Baumester and Diane Tice—came up with several "willpower workout" programs to test with students. They measured each student's current willpower by having them do various self-control tasks, everything from squeezing a handgrip to keeping their hands in ice-cold water as long as possible. This would give each participant a baseline of willpower against which to measure improvements, much like testing a runner's mile time before and after a particular workout program.

The researchers then split the participants into four groups, each of which worked a different willpower component. The first group of students was to exercise their will power by working on their posture. As much as possible, they were to stand or sit up straight, overriding their natural inclinations to hunch or slouch. The second group of students exercised their won't power by attempting to control their emotions. Whenever they felt the impulse to feel bad about something, they were to try to cheer themselves up. The third group of students was to exercise their want power by recording everything they ate in a food journal (when you monitor your diet in this way, you naturally compare what you are eating with what you should be eating, which stimulates the part of the brain responsible for long-term goals). Then they had a control group of participants who did not do any exercises.

After two weeks of doing the willpower workouts, the participants were invited back into the laboratory to assess their progress. They performed the same self-control tasks, and researchers measured their current willpower against their former baselines. The group who worked on their posture turned out to show the greatest improvement. The participants who had spent two weeks rigorously fighting against their natural tendencies to slouch were able to persevere much longer on the tests of willpower than they had previously—and than any of the other groups currently.

The second-biggest improvement came from the group who exercised their want power by monitoring their food. The group who attempted to control their emotions, however, showed no improvement at all. They didn't make any more progress than the control group who did no exercises. In addition to the conclusion that if you do not work your willpower, it will not improve—as the researchers had theorized—this finding also led the research team to the interesting conclusion that regulating emotions does not actually exercise your willpower. You cannot force yourself to be happy.

Above all, this experiment showed once more that willpower really is like a muscle. Not only does it need fuel and rest, but it can also be strengthened through the proper practice. After Muraven's study showed that willpower can be strengthened, other researchers began testing to discover ways we might be able to strengthen our willpower. The best of the methods include:

1) *Meditating.* Meditation has been proven to show the fastest results of any willpower workout. When you meditate, you are training your brain to focus and resist the urge to wander. With practice, this allows you to control your primitive brain more easily and gives your modern brain more influence.

   Research shows that after just two to three days of practicing meditation for ten minutes, your brain will be able to focus better, you will have more energy, and you will be less stressed. Take a look at the next section for a more detailed explanation of how to begin meditating.

2) *Working on your posture.* The second most effective workout is the posture exercise Muraven discovered. This exercise will work especially well on your "willpower stamina," meaning that it will help you increase your ability to exert your willpower over a longer period of time. So even after a long day of work, you will be able to exert more willpower to go to the gym or cook yourself something healthy for dinner.

   To get started, simply correct your posture every time you catch yourself slouching. It sounds extremely simple, but it takes great willpower to sit and stand up straight. Every time you correct your posture, you are essentially doing one "rep" with your willpower muscle. If this seems like too much to do throughout the entire day, choose a set period of time instead. Even doing it for as little as one hour a day for two weeks has been proven to show significant willpower results.

3) *Keeping a food diary.* Most of us do not log the food we eat, so it takes willpower to remember and keep track of it all. This process also helps you become more conscious of the food that you are eating, which will naturally help you eat healthier—leading to even more willpower, as we learned in the last chapter.

   There are multiple apps available that make it extremely easy to log all of your eating information. But if you prefer the old-fashioned way, doing something as simple as keeping a notebook with you and writing down the day, time, and food that you eat will work just fine. Try keeping the diary for just two weeks and see how it increases your ability to resist temptations.

4) *Using your other hand.* Using the same methodology as Muraven, researchers conducted subsequent studies that tested other corrective actions. One practice that worked particularly well was when participants used their non-dominant hand. Your brain is wired to use your dominant hand, so it takes willpower to use your weak one.

   To begin, select about an hour of the day during which to use your non-dominant hand. It does not need to be any more than an hour in order to get results, and in fact, if you aim for more than an hour, you may unnecessarily expend too much of your willpower muscle on this exercise and have less for more important tasks throughout the day.

5) *Correcting your speech.* Another test that researchers conducted was to change subjects' natural speech. For some

this was resisting the urge to use swear words, and for others it was to say "hello" instead of "hey." Again, it takes willpower to consciously go against your instincts. It does not matter how you correct your speech, as long as you change how you habitually talk.

Select a period of the day during which to practice, and think about the words you will change. A simple and effective tactic is to stop using contractions (using "do not" instead of "don't," for example) during work hours. Like with all exercises listed above, doing this for just two weeks can vastly improve your willpower.

6) *Creating and meeting self-imposed deadlines.* Remember what it was like cramming for a test at the last minute in school? Your willpower was taxed as you tried to tune out distractions and become hyper-productive. Researchers found that by creating self-imposed deadlines, you can exercise your willpower in the same way.

Start by picking a task on your to-do list that you may have been putting off. Set a deadline for accomplishing it, and make sure you adhere to that deadline. Remarkably, the participants who set and met deadlines for two weeks not only got their old to-dos done, but also improved their diets, exercised more, and cut back on cigarettes and alcohol.

7) *Keeping track of your spending.* In the same way most of us do not track the food that we eat, many of us do not track our spending either. Researchers found that keeping track of where your money goes will improve your willpower, even if you do not cut back on your purchases.

A great way to begin is to try using a budgeting service. There are plenty available online, many of which can connect to your bank accounts and credit cards to automatically categorize your purchases. As you review your purchases on a regular basis, you will see increases in your focus and ability to resist unrelated temptations like sweets.

8) *Squeezing a handgrip.* If you are truly determined and want to increase your perseverance in a physical way, you can squeeze a handgrip to the point of exhaustion. Squeezing a handgrip creates a deep burn in your forearm, so it will require your willpower to continue squeezing it as long as possible.

9) *Carrying around something tempting.* Again, for the truly determined out there, you can increase your ability to say "no" by carrying around something tempting with you all day. Researchers tried this with participants when teaching them how to resist cravings. After the lesson, they gave each participant a Hershey's Kiss to carry around. Those who were able to resist eating the Kiss were much more capable of resisting other temptations in their lives as well.

10) *Being more conscious of your automatic decisions.* A final exercise is to simply be more mindful of your decisions throughout the day. We are often so lost in thought that our actions become automatic. Taking time to think about your habitual actions will increase your ability to focus and resist temptations.

Try to catch yourself in an automatic behavior and ask yourself why you are doing it. It may be questioning why you are taking the elevator versus the stairs, or it may be questioning why you put two sugars in your coffee. Any way you can think consciously about a typical automatic behavior will increase your focus and self-control.

All of these exercises will help strengthen your willpower, but you should only choose one to use at a time. Doing more than one will overload your willpower muscle and leave it too weak to take on the truly important things in your life, so select the one exercise that is best for you and your goals.

Meditation

As I mentioned above, meditation is perhaps the most powerful exercise for your willpower. Meditation is a practice of some of the most famous and successful people in the world. Jerry Seinfeld, Clint Eastwood, Rupert Murdoch, Paul McCartney, Oprah Winfrey, and many others all spend time each day meditating. But why?

To understand, let's first explore what meditation really is. Meditation is simply the practice of bringing your thoughts to the present moment. Forty-seven percent of our lives is spent either reminiscing about the past or thinking about the future. We spend very little time with a clear mind focused what we are doing *right now.* Meditation is an attempt to bring us to that place.

This is usually accomplished by sitting upright in a room that is clear of distractions and focusing solely on your breathing, but it can be achieved via any activity that brings your full focus and attention to the present. For example, if you are completely focused on the task of cleaning dishes—without mentally going over your day, pondering another problem in your head, or thinking about what you will be doing next—you can achieve a state of meditation. You see the benefits of meditation when your mind is clear and you are focused completely on your present task.

Your brain loves to wander. It loves to think about anything and everything that is exciting. It loves to be undisciplined. During meditation, the goal is to resist these urges. By placing your attention on your breathing, you are training your brain to become more focused and disciplined.

The more you practice resisting your brain's urge to wander, the easier it will be to resist other temptations in your life as well.

Besides increasing your willpower, you will also see the following benefits:

- *Heightened focus.* When you think about your ability to focus, you probably think about being completely engaged in a task. Some people call this a state of "flow." But being focused is just as much about the ability to tune out the distractions around us as it is to engage with what's in front of us. Meditation not only trains your mind to focus on a task, it also trains your ability to tune out distractions.

  For example, when you're working on a project on your computer, you might be tempted to browse the Internet, check your e-mail, look up news stories, and so on. Meditation helps you control these urges and tune out everything except what you should be focused on.

- *Lowered stress.* Much of stress comes from the inability to control thoughts and emotions. You may linger on a painful memory from the past or get anxious about something coming up in the future. These thoughts and feelings cause your body to release a chemical called *cortisol*, which increases your stress.

  Meditation trains your mind to let thoughts like these go. It helps you deal with these feelings and understand that they do not have control over your present condition. The more you train your mind in this way, the less cortisol your body produces, leading to less stress in your life.

- *Improved ability to learn.* Another benefit of meditation is its ability to help you learn and retain information. It is no coincidence that many people claim to come up with their best ideas while meditating. Learning is all about making connections between information you know and information you have just taken in. With a clear mind, you are able to more easily make these connections.

- *Increased energy.* Your best rest will come while you are meditating. Even when you are asleep, your subconscious mind is thinking, creating, and dreaming, which requires your energy and attention. During meditation, however, your mind truly gets to rest. It is challenging to keep your mind focused on the present, but once you get to a state where your brain is not contemplating the past or the future, it will be able to truly relax. This relaxation will revitalize you and give you the mental energy you need to take on the day.

If you have never meditated before, you may want to use a guided meditation tool to get started. There are many applications and files that you can download online, but the one I recommend the most is the Headspace app. It is a comprehensive guided meditation tool that is designed specifically for beginners. I have been using it for a long time now and cannot recommend it enough.

If you would prefer to meditate by yourself, however, here is a meditation exercise you can do from Andi Puddicombe—the founder of Headspace—that will give you all of the same benefits:

1) Go to a quiet room where you can sit upright and where you will not be disturbed.
2) Set a timer for ten minutes, take a seat in a chair, and make sure that you are completely comfortable.
3) Find something in your direct line of vision to focus on, and take six deep breaths. With each exhalation, allow your body to soften as you become more and more relaxed. On the sixth exhalation, gently close your eyes.

4) Focus your attention on the points of contact between your body, the chair, and the floor. Feel the sensation of your arms on the chair and your feet on the floor.

5) Begin to take in the senses of the space around you: any sounds that you hear, any scents that you smell, and so on. Become aware of your surroundings.

6) Turn your attention to your breath. Feel your chest expand as you inhale and contract as you exhale.

7) Once you are comfortable with the rhythm of your breathing, begin to count—"one" on the inhale, "two" on the exhale—all the way up to ten. This will help you to focus your mind on your breathing and prevent it from wandering.

8) When you get to ten, repeat the exercise again from the beginning, at one.

9) As you breathe, allow thoughts to come and go. You cannot stop yourself from thinking, but you can stop your mind from lingering on a thought. The moment you realize that your mind has wandered, simply bring it back to counting breaths.

10) Continue this practice until the timer goes off.

If you are new to meditation, this will be awkward and difficult at first. Do not let that discourage you. I like to think about it like learning to drive a car. At first, there are so many things going on that you feel overwhelmed, and the ride is bumpy and awkward. But over time, you start getting more used to it. Driving becomes more automatic, and the ride becomes smoother. This same thing will occur with meditation if you give it time.

Meditation is one of the most simple and effective ways to strengthen your willpower. By meditating for ten minutes per day, you improve your willpower, focus, energy, and learning ability while also becoming less stressed. After just one week, you should see some significant results.

But even if you choose a willpower workout other than meditation, you will see the benefits. There is incredible value to all of the exercises listed. However, sometimes training is not enough. According to Blaine, his deliberate willpower practice was only good enough to get him through the first fifty-five hours in the ice. The last eight hours required something different. They required a mental exercise that can instantly boost your willpower: chunking.

Instantly Boost Your Willpower

"What time is it?" Blaine asked a man he saw on the other side of the ice.

"It's two o'clock," the man responded.

That's when Blaine remembered that the prime-time finale was scheduled for ten o'clock, meaning he had eight hours left in the block of ice. His first thought was one of complete devastation. He couldn't believe that he still had so far to go. How could he motivate himself through those excruciating last hours?

Okay, he thought to himself, *I just need to make it through the next two hours. Then it will only be six hours left. And that won't be so bad.*

That's it. That's how Blaine was able to make it through the torture he was facing. He could not fathom having to stay encased in that block of ice for a full working day. So he broke it into what he believed he *could* do: two hours. He knew he could make it through the next two hours. This change in perspective immediately strengthened his willpower because now he was focused on a goal that was attainable. When he hit that two-hour mark, he then broke up the remaining six hours into even smaller chunks. Blaine endured chunk after chunk until he finally made it to his release.

Blaine is not the only hero to use this chunking technique. As you may recall, Joe De Sena did not just run Ironman triathlons, he also ran a 100-mile ultramarathon. When asked how he was able to endure those miles with an injured hip, Joe responded, "I'm really good at compartmentalizing. If you're 10 miles into a 100-

mile run and you're thinking about mile 90, you're dead. You've got to think about mile 11 and completely shut out the next twenty-four hours."

Joe knew that focusing on the huge goal of the 100 miles was only going to demotivate him. He didn't know if he could make it through the whole thing. But he did know that he could make it through the next mile, so that is what he focused on. Just like David Blaine, he simply completed one chunk after the next until finally he had completed all 100 miles.

How Chunking Works

When you focus your attention on a task, you probably tend to think about the whole landscape of things that need to be done. You focus on "the cathedral" rather than simply "laying each brick."

This sounds good in theory. After all, you want to be able to see the big picture. However, when you focus on the cathedral, your brain gets overwhelmed with how much work you need to do to build it. You think about just how far away you are from reaching your goal, rather than focusing on the steps needed to get there. You see "mile ninety" rather than focusing on just getting through "mile eleven." When you do this, you actually drain your willpower as your brain expends mental energy thinking about all that needs to be done.

This also makes each step that you take toward your goal seem insignificant. Compared to the cathedral that you have in your mind, each brick that you lay down has little impact on the overall picture. At best, this will leave you feeling discouraged, as it seems like you are making little to no progress. At worst, it will lead you to take shortcuts and try a quick-fix plan that will be unsustainable.

It benefits you far more to focus your attention solely on what you need to do next. In doing so, you will strengthen your willpower with each step in the right direction. Below you will find the key reasons why chunking is so effective:

- *Each chunk you complete represents a small win.* Small wins are greater than their benefits on paper. With each small win, you grow confidence that you can get another, perhaps even larger, win next time. For example, when most people set a goal to lose weight by exercising, they focus on the overall weight loss goal rather than on completing each workout. That makes each workout seem insignificant compared to the larger goal. After all, one workout will hardly make a difference—leading you to become frustrated about your lack of instant results.

  However, if you focus your attention on simply accomplishing your workout, you will gain confidence with each trip to the gym. You will start being able to lift heavier weights, run farther distances, and crave the endorphin rush that you get from physical exercise. Focusing on the chunk reframes your perspective to enjoy the process, enjoy completing each chunk, and enjoy each small win on the way to your goal.

- *You complete each chunk with a higher level of quality.* By focusing on each mile, Joe De Sena was able to compare his current with his previous mile time and make it a fun competition. With each mile, he wanted to continue to improve his pace. But if he focused on the full 100 miles, the quality of each individual mile would seem irrelevant.

  Shifting your focus to each chunk individually changes this perspective. If you focus your attention on each individual workout, you will push yourself much harder. It will become less of a chore because you will care about lifting heavier weights or running more miles than in your previous workouts. Eventually, the by-product of each individual workout will be the larger goal of becoming a healthier person.

- *It helps you stay in the present.* One of the biggest problems you can face with willpower is imagining future pain. You envision the pain you will endure over the whole 100-mile race and unnecessarily burden yourself early. You will only make your present situation worse by thinking about how far you are from the finish line. Joe De Sena may have endured pain in his eleventh mile, but if he had thought about the pain of the next ninety miles as well, he would have endured much more.

Many people skip workouts because they envision future pain and exhaustion. Whenever you are stressed or tired, you are prone to believe that exerting yourself in the future will be painful. This process drains your willpower and makes it even harder to stick to your workout plan. But if you stay in the present and focus just on what you need to do next, you will increase your likelihood of conquering your goals. Instead of thinking about what you will do in the gym, focus on having a pre-workout snack. Then focus on putting on your gym clothes. Then focus on walking to your car. Each step is simple and easy when you stay in the present.

The first question that many people want to ask when they learn about chunking is what size each chunk should be. The answer is that it depends on you and what you are chunking. A good general rule is that each chunk should be large enough to get a small win, but small enough that you won't feel overwhelmed. And if your goal is larger than a single task, you can follow the chunking method that was created by Alcoholics Anonymous: "Do not have a drink *today.*" Do not focus on the ninety-day diet or the eight-week exercise program—focus your willpower on simply accomplishing your goal *today.* This will make the task seem much less daunting and, before you know it, days, weeks, and months of success will go by.

Working Out for the Long Term

Now that you have in your arsenal all of these techniques for working out your willpower in the short term, you may be wondering what the best way is to ultimately change your behavior for the long term. You're trying to be more consistent with the behaviors that will help you achieve your long-term goals. When you set a plan to engage in deliberate practice, you want to achieve it—not just tomorrow, but for the foreseeable future.

Many people believe that the best way to change long-term behavior is by developing habits. But the truth is that, while habits can be powerful tools, they have a big downside that can cause them to backfire: They are formed in the primitive brain. By trying to design habits, you're essentially delegating your long-term goals to your short-term brain, which also leads to strengthening your primitive brain rather than your modern brain.

So if not by using habits, how do you change your behavior? The best way to begin is by delegating your long-term goals to the modern brain, then using everything you've learned in this chapter to strengthen it. Your modern brain is your ultimate decision-maker. It has the capacity to choose the thing you really want to do even when that choice is hard. Research by McGonigal has shown that there are several strategies you can use to make sticking to the behaviors that you want more automatic within your modern brain:

1) *Automate your goal dedication.* Automating your goal dedication is about setting triggers and reminders of your overall goal. This could be following a plan to write down your goals every day, sending yourself goal reminders, or increasing your self-awareness.

When you are automating your goal pursuit, it is helpful to come up with simple rules to help you achieve your goals. For example, if you are trying to maintain healthy eating habits at a cocktail party, a simple rule like "only eat the healthiest things there," "be mindful of how much you are eating throughout the night," or "keep track of everything you eat and drink in a food diary" can help keep you on track. You can create a plan and use your willpower to execute it.

2) *Make mindful decisions.* The simple but conscious decisions to resist temptations, go for a run, or ensure you study at least one hour per day all strengthen your modern brain. Be mindful of the decisions that you need to make in order to reach your goals. With every choice that you make today to work toward a better tomorrow, you will also be strengthening your willpower.

3) *Make commitments.* When you get into a relationship with someone, you make a commitment. You remain faithful to that person even if someone else tempts you from time to time because you believe in the greater purpose of the relationship. This same principle holds true for your goals as well. In many cases you don't need to have a specific behavioral response to avoid a temptation; you just need a higher purpose, whether that is your health, being a good role model for your kids, or a dream to believe in. Making a commitment to your goal will help you deal with challenges that arise. This commitment will spring your want power into action and give you motivation to act on your long-term aspirations.

You are constantly faced with different scenarios that will challenge your focus on your long-term goals. When this occurs, your best shot at success is to be mindful of the situation and think about how you can make a decision that is consistent with what you really want in life—actions taken by your modern brain. In the end, it is this part of the brain that determines your ultimate success, so it benefits you to give it as much power as possible. To get through his horrendous experience in the ice, David Blaine did not fall back on the impulses of his primitive brain. He used deliberate practice to slowly but surely strengthen his modern brain until he was strong enough to endure that torture for hours on end.

Conclusion

David Blaine has reached a level of willpower that many of us can only dream about. He is truly able to push the limits of what the human body and mind are capable of accomplishing. But his story reveals that he is not inhuman. He faced real pain and suffering in that block of ice; his success was a result of his strengthening his willpower to a point where he was capable of accomplishing such a tremendous feat.

But Blaine is not the only one with the capability of strengthening his willpower. The work of various researchers has highlighted proven exercises that you can do on a regular basis to strengthen your own willpower. Working out your willpower in the short term and powering up your modern brain in the long term will give you the strength you need to achieve your goals.

Key Points

- *Your willpower can be strengthened.* David Blaine was able to accomplish his incredible stunts because he strengthened his willpower muscle through training.

- *The best way to strengthen your willpower is through meditation.* Meditation is the fastest, simplest, and most effective way to strengthen your willpower. Research shows that after just three days of meditating for ten minutes per day, you will see results.

- *Chunking will instantly strengthen your willpower.* Your brain is easily overwhelmed. When you focus on the big goal, you can become disheartened by how much work it will take to achieve. You can reverse this effect, though, by breaking your goal into manageable chunks.

- *Willpower is mind-full, habits are mind-less.* Designing habits can backfire on you because they are formed in the primitive brain. This will cause you to strengthen your primitive brain instead of your modern brain. With your long-term goals, you want to be mind-full, not mind-less.

Strategies

1) *Meditate for ten minutes per day.* Begin a practice of daily meditation. For the best results, make this a part of your morning routine.

2) *Choose a willpower workout.* Once you're comfortable meditating regularly, choose one of the willpower workouts to do. Focus on consistency, not intensity.

3) *Break your huge tasks into manageable chunks.* Each chunk should be large enough to serve as a small win, yet small enough to not be overwhelming.

4) *Automate your goal dedication.* Instead of automating your behavior through habits, automate your dedication by having a set of rules to guide your behavior.

5) *Commit to your higher goal.* Make a commitment to your higher goal in the same way you would commit to a spouse. By reinforcing that commitment, you will strengthen it.

Part III

Using Willpower

Chapter 5

Finding Your Purpose

"I know the goal. And whatever it takes to get there, I will do."
– Arnold Schwarzenegger

Growing up in rural Austria, Arnold Schwarzenegger had little chance of achieving fame or fortune. He lived in a tiny village called Thal, where children were groomed to follow in their parents' footsteps. Arnold's parents were set on him joining the military and becoming a police officer like his father. However, unlike other kids his age, Arnold was set on bigger things than life in Thal.

One day, Arnold picked up a magazine with the world bodybuilding champion, Reg Park, on the cover. He flipped through the magazine and found Park's story, titled "How Mr. Universe Became Hercules." As he read the story, the vision became clear: Arnold was going to be just like Reg Park. He was going to become a bodybuilding champion and a huge movie star.

To his family and friends, this was crazy. Few people even knew what bodybuilding was back then—especially in a rural Austrian village. Yet despite their ridicule, Arnold began lifting weights like a madman. Although he only had access to a gym with poor equipment, he spent hours every day getting stronger. He didn't have a formal coach to design his deliberate practice, but he did have the instruction of older boys who lifted weights. After years of hard work, he became the most muscular student at his high school and competed in several small, local weight-lifting events.

Despite his best efforts, however, Arnold was still forced to follow his father's wishes. When he turned eighteen, he was sent off to the military. This devastated Arnold but did not hold him back from following his vision. When he entered the military, he told himself, *Okay, Arnold, you know the goal. Whatever it takes to get there, you will do.* And he meant it.

Military life was harsh, especially for an aspiring bodybuilder. After running with heavy boots at five o'clock in the morning, cleaning guns, going to the shooting range, marching several miles, climbing up hills with weapons, and watching his fellow recruits fall dead asleep at night, Arnold did an extra three hours of strength training. This was especially difficult because he didn't have access to the proper equipment. He had to work with what was at hand; chairs, bars, ropes—whatever he could find he made into an exercise. Then he woke up early the next morning to do push-ups, chin-ups, and sit-ups before the mandatory five o'clock run.

This relentless effort only made Arnold look insane. Everybody around him made fun of his dream. They scoffed at the work he was putting in and tried to snap him out of his fantasy world. But Arnold tuned them all out. He had his vision, and he was going to make it reality.

Then he finally got the chance he'd waited for his whole life. He was invited to compete in the Junior Mr. Europe championship in Stuttgart, Germany. Unfortunately, this was also his *only* chance. Once he passed the age of eighteen, he could no longer qualify for junior-level events. And without competing in one of those, he might never be invited to a competition at the next level.

Of course, the military would not grant him leave to go to the competition. To make it there, Arnold knew he must devise a plan to sneak off of the base. But if he was caught, the consequences were severe. He might get sanctions, weeks of solitary confinement, or even years in prison. For the first time in his life, Arnold was seriously questioning how badly he wanted to achieve his vision.

Was it really worth it? What if it was just a crazy fantasy? Then Arnold remembered the magazine he'd picked up as a boy.

He remembered that Reg Park had done it, so it was possible. The decision became clear: He had to go.

Arnold waited until nighttime, jumped over an unlit fence, and left the base. Without any transportation of his own, he had to hop freight trains to get to Stuttgart. He rode the trains for twenty-six straight hours before finally arriving in Stuttgart on the morning of the competition. He was still dressed in his military uniform, and he had to borrow trunks from one of the earlier competitors mere minutes before taking the stage.

All of these factors would have left many people flustered, but Arnold seized his moment. He showed extraordinary confidence and poise while on stage and drew huge cheers from the crowd. This landed Arnold in the final three competitors—he was so close. After another round of posing, Arnold waited patiently as the judges gave their rankings. They announced third place, second place, and the winner: Arnold Schwarzenegger.

He was in utter disbelief. He had been right this whole time; he really could become a bodybuilding champion. That victory was the small win Arnold needed to launch the massive success that followed. From there, he won competition after competition, including the top prize, Mr. Olympia, six years in a row. He became the best thing to happen to bodybuilding before completing his vision by becoming one of the great action stars of the twentieth century. And this all happened because he never lost sight of what he knew was possible.

Throughout his whole journey to success, Arnold was fueled by one thing: his purpose. He knew what was possible. That purpose not only helped him overcome the pressure to conform, but also the thousands of hours of hard physical training it took to make his dream come true. It takes a lot of willpower to push through both of those challenges, so let's examine exactly how Arnold's vision gave him the willpower to achieve greatness.

Search for Purpose

Before he even picked up the magazine about Reg Park, Arnold knew that he had to get out of that little Austrian village. He knew that his purpose in life was something beyond becoming a police officer, marrying a girl in Thal, and living the simple life. He wanted something more. So he began a search for his purpose.

He may not have realized it, but because he was dreaming of a life beyond the fields of Thal, his brain began searching for the way out. So when he did come upon that magazine with Reg Park, his mind was ready for the plan. Undoubtedly, plenty of children in tiny villages around the world also picked up that magazine. But they saw it from a different perspective than Arnold. They did not see a plan, simply because they were not looking for one. The plan was so clear to Arnold because his brain was in search of a solution to a problem.

The first step in the journey to greatness is not to have a vision; it is to open your mind up to the search. It is okay if you do not know what you really want in life yet; you only must be willing to find it. When you open your mind, your brain will subconsciously start looking for your purpose. You will open yourself up to clues and signs that indicate you may be on the right path. You may find your purpose in something you read or in some line of work that you attempt. But the important thing is that you begin the search. Because once you find that purpose, you will find more willpower than you knew you had.

The Power of Purpose

The civil rights movement of the 1950s and 1960s serves as one of the greatest examples of how powerful a great purpose can be. African-Americans, who had never been treated as equals in the entire history of the American South, finally said "enough." They stood tall and declared that it was time to stop being treated as second-class citizens. It was time to stop being abused for the sake of their skin color, and it was time to end the oppression they had faced for centuries. And the catalyst for the entire movement was one simple seamstress who would not give up her seat on a bus to a white passenger.

Rosa Parks' simple act of defiance was the spark that the National Association for the Advancement of Colored People needed to move the African-American community to action. Her story inspired thousands to risk losing their jobs, to risk endangering their families, and to risk their very way of life to become a part of a movement that had little chance of success. The people who first began protesting in the civil rights movement risked everything they held dear in order to fight for a purpose greater than themselves.

And it did not stop there. A brilliant orator by the name of Martin Luther King Jr. became the leader of the movement and not only inspired thousands to join the radical cause, but inspired them to do so through peaceful protest. Imagine the willpower needed to not only take on that much risk, but to resist fighting back against oppressively violent communities.

Through it all, Parks and King continued to inspire more and more people to join them—to potentially lose everything, including their own lives, in order to peacefully fight for the greater purpose of equal opportunities for everyone. Each participant in the movement was able to reach a level of willpower and determination that many of us can only dream of—all because of a great purpose.

How Purpose Changes Perspective

These stories show us the power of purpose at both the individual and the organizational levels. Compared to Arnold's struggle to spend three hours doing strength training every night after a full day of military training, our daily struggle to eat healthy and make it to the gym for thirty minutes seems like nothing. Compared to the risks taken by those who stood in peaceful protest, our worries about making a sales call seem completely insignificant—it's all about perspective.

That is the powerful impact purpose can have on your willpower. It can completely change your perspective, so that you view the struggle and hardships you must face as insignificant compared to what you are fighting for.

When it comes down to it, many of the decisions that you make depend on your perspective of the situation. By now you know that doing something as simple as changing how you say "no" to a temptation can lower your craving for it. You know that saying you "get to" do something rather than you "have to" do something will make it more enjoyable. In the same way, if you see the monotony of your daily deliberate practice as insignificant compared to your purpose and the goal you are working toward, you will be far more likely to achieve it.

Find Your Inspiration

When Arnold read the Reg Park article, he got a burst of inspiration. He was able to see that Reg Park came from humble beginnings, yet still built himself into the most muscular man in the world before becoming a huge movie star.

This inspiration not only gave Arnold the plan for his vision, but it also kept him going through the tough times. When everyone was telling him to give up, he could turn to Park's story and remember that he was not crazy—it really was possible.

You have probably experienced the feeling of inspiration at some point in your life. It may have been from a story on the news, something in history, a speech by a great leader, or the words of someone close to you. When you get this burst of inspiration, you get a rush of energy that makes you feel like you can reach new heights. Like the power of a great purpose, the power of true inspiration provides you with more willpower than you knew you were capable of possessing. But what actually happens in your brain when you get this feeling of inspiration?

Researchers tested this to see what was happening in the brains of people who were inspired. They had participants watch an inspirational speech and ran a scan on their brains to see which areas activated. Sure enough, the area of the modern brain that is responsible for your want power lit up. The neurons in this part of the brain started firing, and the participants felt a rush of willpower as they began to believe in their dreams and goals.

These results prove that inspiration leads to more want power. It makes it easier for you to think, decide, and act on what you really want in life—even without any exercises to strengthen your willpower, without giving your willpower more fuel, and without breaking up necessary tasks into manageable chunks. None of those tactics can give you as much willpower as the right inspiration from a hero.

In fact, almost every great story of sheer willpower you have heard so far began with inspiration. Kobe Bryant scored zero points in his basketball camp at the age of twelve and thought about giving up basketball forever. But then he turned to Michael Jordan's story of getting cut from his high school basketball team, which inspired Kobe to work even harder than Michael did to make it to the NBA. Joe De Sena was frozen and exhausted in Quebec with more than 150 miles to go. Then he thought of Ernest Shackleton's struggles, which gave him the strength to endure. And Tim Grover was inspired by the incredible value of taking big risks when his father moved his family from India to Chicago with nothing more than twenty dollars in his pocket. If his father could do that, then Grover could work with the greatest basketball player in the world.

In this book, you've learned many tactics you can use to give yourself more willpower—and there are still many to come—but there is no better way to achieve great things than through an inspiring purpose.

Positive Thinking

With all of the talk of purpose, inspiration, and how they affect your brain, you may be wondering about the role of positive thinking. After all, Arnold must have reinforced his vision with a lot of positive thinking in order to ignore the naysayers and reach the level of success that he did. So let's discuss the science of positive thinking in achieving your purpose.

The power of positive thinking first emerged when researchers discovered the "law of attraction." This law states that your brain interprets what you visualize in the same way that it interprets what you actually see with your eyes; that is, if you visualize success, your brain will genuinely believe that you are successful. The theory, then, is that by visualizing these positive outcomes, your brain will subtly motivate you to actually attain them. The more you believe you will be successful, the closer you come to actually achieving success.

As a result, people have been instructed to visualize themselves in the career they want, to visualize themselves with the things they want, and to visualize themselves living the life they want. But will this technique really give you the willpower to attain these things?

Researcher Gabriele Oettingen gives us the answer: "Just because you're a dreamer, doesn't mean you're a doer."

Oettingen has been studying the brain and motivation for over twenty years, with a heavy focus on the effects of positive thinking, and she has come to some very different conclusions in her work. In one ingenious experiment, Oettingen and her colleagues had a group of participants come into the laboratory in a dehydrated state. They made each participant sit a room for an extended period of time by himself or herself.

One group of participants was to sit there patiently waiting, while the second group was to visualize themselves drinking an ice-cold glass of water. To the researchers' amazement, the bodily reaction of each participant who visualized herself drinking was as if she had indeed drunk a glass of water. The participants' thirst was quenched, and their bodies were satisfied.

This was an astonishing finding for sure, but that was not the key takeaway from the study. After the initial exercise, both groups were put through a set of challenging tasks to earn an actual glass of water. The participants who had already visualized drinking the water didn't work as hard for the actual water because they didn't need to. Their thirst was already quenched. Oettingen's conclusion, therefore, was that positive visualization does indeed make you believe that you are already in possession of the thing you want—so what is your motivation to work for it?

The law of attraction is a real thing. By visualizing success, you will indeed begin to see yourself in possession of it. But the scientific evidence is yet to prove that visualization makes you more likely to actually attain the thing you seek because, as Oettingen proved, what is the motivation to work for something you believe you already have? If the leaders of the civil rights movement had simply visualized a world where they were treated equally, would they have had the motivation to take the hosing, beating, and torment that they endured in order to make their dream of equality a reality?

We will never know for sure, but as you can see, there is scientific evidence that shows that positive thinking is not effective without actual action to back it up. It is only taking positive action that will lead to successful outcomes. There is no debate about whether engaging in deliberate practice, strengthening your willpower, or working hard will lead to successful outcomes.

Positive action is real. And it will lead to success if you are willing to put in the effort to stop visualizing your reality and start working on creating it.

Beware Inspiration without Action

Just like with positive thinking, there is something to beware with inspiration. If you use inspiration only to visualize the future, rather than to motivate you to take action toward it, you will fall into the same trap as positive thinking without action. As you learned, your brain is so good at visualization that you can probably see extremely vividly your future self with the results that you're trying to get. When you visualize your future self, you risk getting a false sense of reward, as if that success has already happened for you. And when you get that sense of reward, you risk losing the motivation to actually take action toward it.

You are especially susceptible to making this mistake when you first set out to accomplish your goals. When you get inspired to make a big change in your life, there is a big temptation to set an unrealistic plan to accomplish it. After all, big changes are coming, and with big changes, you want big results! And to get big results, you need big efforts.

While you may be able to keep this up for a few days, weeks, or even months, eventually you will run out of steam. Then you may lose hope when you realize how much work you still need to do in order to reach your big goals.

Think about the last time you set a New Year's resolution. You were probably extremely excited as you wrote down all of the goals that you had for the upcoming year. It was a fun process as you visualized what the "new you" would look like after a full year of diet and exercise. You imagined how much more money you would have now that you had the discipline to avoid those impulse purchases. All of this visualization left you feeling optimistic, self-confident, and happy.

But then the monotonous work came. It was cold, and the last thing you wanted to do was get up early and run. You were stressed from a full day of work, and the take-out menu looked a lot more enticing than the prospect of cooking a healthy meal. Your favorite store was having a sale, and you just had to take advantage. Once those difficult choices came, that inspiration and motivation you once had were nowhere to be found.

It is in those moments when you need to take action that inspiration matters the most. Not when you are visualizing your goals for the year, but when you are working toward them. Not right after you sign up for your gym membership, but when you are one month into it and the last thing you want to do is work out. In those moments, remember the greater purpose that you are working toward. Remember the person who inspires you. Remember why you set those goals in the first place, and find your inspiration to make them happen. Remember the reason that you are going through these tough times, and you *will* find the strength to persevere toward what you really want.

Belief

When Arnold was forced to enlist in the military, he had little chance of ever making it as a professional bodybuilder. His dream was essentially dead. Given the reality of having to exert his body for twelve hours a day doing military training—which doesn't help much with bodybuilding—how could he expect to compete? The answer, as we know, is by spending three hours per night doing strength training *after* all of the military training was over. And to push his body through that torture, Arnold did indeed use the power of positive thinking. But he used it much differently than the law of attraction prescribes.

To endure his hours of training, Arnold needed to genuinely believe in the end of his story. He needed to believe that going through this training would lead to his dream coming true.

At the same time, however, he needed to never let the belief that he would become a bodybuilder cloud his view of reality. The reality of his situation was bleak. The brutal fact was that he didn't have much of a chance, so he needed that much deliberate practice in order to have a shot at making it. He embraced the paradox of having faith that in the end he would succeed while still confronting the brutal facts of his reality. And that is what you must do as well.

In order to achieve great things, you must genuinely believe that great things are possible. You must genuinely believe that you will be successful in the end. That is the only way you will be able to tap into your want power and find the strength to endure the journey. At the same time, however, you must not let this faith in the end result cloud your vision of the present. You must confront the brutal facts of your reality, and be willing to fight through them. You must not allow your optimism to cause you to underestimate just how hard it will be to reach your goals.

Arnold had to believe he would be a bodybuilding champion, but he also had to confront the fact that it would take every ounce of strength and energy he had. The civil rights leaders needed to believe they would reach equality, but they had to confront the fact that they would lose much that they held dear along the way.

Use the power of positive thinking to get to the point where you genuinely believe that you can achieve your goals. But once you get to that point, you need to stop visualizing and start acting.

Conclusion

Arnold Schwarzenegger had virtually no chance of achieving any level of fame or fortune in his life. He grew up in a world where bodybuilding was unheard of and Hollywood was half a world away. Despite his situation, however, Arnold never lost faith that one day he would become a bodybuilding champion and a huge movie star.

Like the other heroes in this book, he did not get there through talent, through luck, or through solely visualizing himself there. Ultimately, he got there because he had the willpower to follow through with his vision. He had the mental strength to ignore the peer pressure to conform and to push his body to its limit.

He was able to use a higher purpose, to use a vision, and to use raw inspiration as the energy and motivation to push him when things got hard. But ultimately, he became a great bodybuilder and action star because he wasn't a dreamer—he was a doer. A vision will get you started, but purpose is required to keep you going.

Key Points

- *Your purpose is your greatest source of willpower.* A great purpose is the best way to tap into your want power. Your brain will give you more motivation and energy to achieve a goal if you truly believe that it is worth it.

- *A hero will help you stay committed.* When Arnold questioned if his dream was possible, he could turn to his hero Reg Park. A hero like that will give you inspiration and belief, even on the worst days.

- *Positive thinking may actually be a detriment you.* The law of attraction will make you genuinely believe you are in possession of what you visualize, and that may make you less willing to work for it.

- *Beware of inspiration without action.* Inspiration is far more important in the middle of reaching your goals than it is in the beginning. Use your inspiration to find motivation when you're three months into achieving a goal—that's when you need it.

Strategies

1) *Search for a purpose.* If you don't know your purpose yet, simply open your mind up to the search.

2) *Find your inspiration.* Who has reached your purpose before? Learn how they got there, what obstacles they faced, and how they overcame them.

3) *Focus on positive action.* Believe you can reach your purpose, but understand the action you must take to achieve it.

Chapter 6

Becoming Gritty

"It is our choices that show what we truly are, far more than our abilities."
– J.K. Rowling

The idea seemed to come out of nowhere. There was nothing special or magical around her. It was simply a train ride from Manchester to London to most of the passengers. But for one passenger, it would be the spark that set her on the path to becoming the world's first billionaire author. Joanne Rowling—better known as J.K. Rowling, author of the *Harry Potter* series—was overcome with excitement as she came up with an idea that would change the literary world.

"I saw Harry! I could see him very clearly—this scrawny little boy. And it was the most physical rush of excitement. I've never felt that physical reaction to anything about writing before. It was the same feeling that you get when you meet someone new and feel as if you have found the person you are going to spend the rest of your life with."

She could hardly contain her joy, even as she regretted the fact that she didn't have a pen and paper with her to write down her ideas. So she just sat there, thinking about this new world that would contain Hogwarts, Azkaban, and the full cast of characters that countless people would soon fall deeply in love with.

That love, however, would not come for many years. And the journey from that initial idea to the publication of the first *Harry Potter* book would be filled with pain, suffering, and depression.

Sometime after that fateful ride from Manchester, Rowling married a man and moved with him to Portugal. After the birth of their daughter Jessica, however, the marriage turned sour and Rowling returned to the United Kingdom with Jessica to live in Edinburgh. There, as she continued to build the world of Harry Potter, her own world continued to fall apart. As the single parent of a newborn baby, she could not even get a job. As she said, "Anyone who has ever seen what state-run child care is like will understand why I wouldn't put my daughter in their hands during the day."

Thus, Rowling had to live on welfare while she worked on the book and cared for her infant child. Rowling was so exhausted that she could not even muster the energy to do housework. After a long day of writing and caring for Jessica, her willpower muscle was too weak to care. This left her in a constant battle with depression, as she wondered if Harry was worth it.

"I had to fight my realistic side. I was a first-time author, so of course I was going to struggle to get published. And just because I thought the story was great didn't mean everyone else would. To muster the willpower to keep writing, I had to truly believe in Harry. I knew he was bigger than me. I knew I had to do right by this book."

Doing right didn't just mean writing a story from start to finish. Rowling went above and beyond for Harry. She wrote down the name, house, and magical powers of *every single student* at Hogwarts. She wrote down each magical spell and its use. She drew all the major characters and scenes in the book to make them more real to her. She was meticulous in crafting each aspect of the story. Her living conditions may not have been perfect, but the world of Harry Potter was going to be.

After five long years, Rowling finally finished the book. Then she began a new struggle: trying to get someone to publish her.

Luckily, she found an agent who would be her loyal partner, as he truly believed in Rowling and truly believed in Harry.

"We were very excited about the book," said Christopher Little, Rowling's literary agent, "but it was very difficult to sell. Quite a large number of big publishing houses turned it down. They believed it was too long for children and not politically correct."

After being turned down by twelve of the best names in publishing, Little and Rowling finally found one that was willing to give Harry a chance. For a meager $4,000, Bloomsbury Publishing bought the rights to *Harry Potter*—and then promptly told Rowling that, although they liked the book, she should start looking for full-time work. The book simply did not have enough "commercial appeal." Believing every word, Rowling went back to work as an English teacher, as Jessica was now old enough to attend school.

Finally, after working through all the steps of the publishing process, Rowling received word that Harry was now on shelves for readers to purchase. This news gave her the most elated feeling she'd ever had. As she described it, "My only lifetime ambition had just been fulfilled. I could not believe that I was actually going to be in print."

Of course, once Harry hit the shelves, he became an instant hit. *Harry Potter and the Philosopher's Stone* became so big, in fact, that US publishers started a bidding war for American rights to the book. Eventually, Scholastic bought the rights for $105,000—more than they had ever paid any author, let alone a first-time author. After entering the US market, the book became an international sensation. Then the rest, as they say, is history.

To get to that point of success, however, Rowling had to show great passion and perseverance as she worked toward a very specific long-term goal. In other words, she had grit.

What Is Grit?

Angela Duckworth realized that she had her work cut out for her. She had just left her management-consulting job to begin teaching math to seventh-graders in a New York City public school. Like most teachers, she entered the classroom with the thought that her most intelligent students would also be the ones who were most successful. But for some reason, many of her brightest students were struggling, while many of her strongest performers were not her smartest. So what was it exactly that made her students perform well? What was the true factor in their success?

This question led Duckworth to go back to graduate school and begin investigating what the real factors of success were in many different academic settings. She studied what distinguished different successes, from students winning the National Spelling Bee, to college graduates being top of their class at West Point, to teachers getting through to kids in tough neighborhoods.

She found an underlying factor of success that was applicable across all these very different domains. The people who had the highest IQs, the most prestigious academic backgrounds, or the highest family income were *not* the most successful. The success stories, she found, were those people with the most grit.

Grit is passion and perseverance while working toward a specific long-term goal. It is the ability to work toward this goal day in and day out—not just for days or weeks, but for years. It is Kobe Bryant working relentlessly to become a great basketball player. It is Arnold Schwarzenegger lifting more weights than anyone in Thal from the time he was a young boy. And it is J.K. Rowling pushing herself through terrible times to share Harry with the world.

Regardless of how talented you are, or how many resources you have at your disposal, nothing will lead you to success as much as grit. In fact, in her research, Duckworth actually found that talent was either irrelevant to success or detrimental to success. Why? It is because those who were the most talented tended to rest on their talent, meaning that they did not develop the strong work ethic necessary to stick with something for long enough to be gritty.

The Difference Between Grit and Willpower

Duckworth's findings probably do not come as too much of a surprise to you at this point. After all, essentially all of the heroes we have come across in this book have shown these gritty traits. Aren't we really just talking about willpower again? Even by J.K. Rowling's own admittance, it took "willpower" for her to ignore her realistic self and continue writing *Harry Potter*. So what is the difference grit and willpower?

To explain, I'll use an example from my own life. Before embarking on the research project that led to the creation of this book, I was working as a marketing consultant, competing at an elite level in Spartan Races, and reading about the science of willpower on the side. And I used my own willpower to be extremely disciplined in pursuing each of these three aspects of my life.

I woke up every day at four o'clock in the morning, ate a healthy breakfast, worked out from five to seven, got to the office before anyone else, worked diligently all day, and learned about the science of willpower at night. It was a tough schedule, but I knew about a lot of those willpower-building tactics, and I strengthened my willpower to the point where I could handle it all. But while my willpower was strong, I wasn't very gritty.

In pursuing all three of those goals at once, I wasn't making much progress in any of them. I was an above-average marketer, I was finishing around tenth place in all of the Spartan Races I was competing in, and I wrote one blog post per month for about 100 subscribers I'd built up over two years—all signs of some success, certainly, but not signs of greatness. Despite all of my willpower, I was *good* at three things, but I was not *great* at anything.

I decided it was time to focus. I needed to choose my one, singular purpose. Did I want to be a great marketer? Did I want to be a great athlete? Or did I want to be a great researcher and writer of performance psychology?

Once I forced myself to make a choice, the answer was obvious. And once I focused all of my time, creativity, and willpower on becoming a great researcher and writer of performance psychology, everything else started falling into place. I was learning more insightful things, I was becoming a better writer, and I was coming closer to achieving greatness in my own right. Meanwhile, my number of subscribers doubled, then tripled, then quadrupled, and less than a year after I focused in, I had over 30,000 people following my blog.

To use an analogy, think of greatness as chopping down a tree and willpower as the ax. When I was focusing on three different pursuits, I was chopping at the tree in three different places—using a lot of willpower, but not making much actual progress toward greatness. But when I got gritty and focused on only one pursuit, I started chopping the tree in the same place every time. And with the same number of swings from the willpower ax, I was on a much faster route to greatness.

Duckworth encountered this same phenomenon in her research, when she examined the people who were extraordinarily successful in life versus those who were only successful in school. Students with a lot of willpower had very high GPAs, just like students with a lot of grit. However, the students with only willpower did not become nearly as successful in life as their gritty counterparts. The gritty ones were those who had a vision of what they wanted in life and used their willpower to pursue it with excellence. Meanwhile, the ones with only willpower tried one domain for a while, decided it wasn't for them, then tried another domain, then another—never achieving greatness in anything.

How to Become Gritty

So how do you become gritty? How do you develop such deep belief in what you are doing that you are willing to persevere through things like poverty and depression even without a realistic shot at reaching success?

Unfortunately, there is no hard scientific answer to these questions. You cannot force yourself to have a purpose that drives you to push through that kind of adversity. If you do not truly believe in the thing you are fighting for, then you are simply not going to have the strength to endure this painful process for the long term.

That is why grit comes after purpose. You must first have your vision of what you want to accomplish in your mind before you develop the grit to pursue it all the way to completion. After you have your "aha moment," like J.K. Rowling had on the train and Arnold Schwarzenegger had when he read the story of Reg Park, you must be comfortable focusing your willpower on that one thing.

Many people have had ideas as good as—or even better than—Rowling's. But she was successful because she was so passionate about sharing the story of Harry Potter with the world that she was willing to endure whatever it took to get her book on bookshelves. She focused her willpower on that very specific long-term goal, and she refused to give up during the most difficult part of any journey—the middle.

The Middle

It was four o'clock in the morning on January 6, and Chicago was being hit by what was called the "Polar Vortex," where northern cities across the United States were hitting record-low temperatures. With the wind chill, it was a reported negative forty degrees Fahrenheit. Like many people across the country, just one week earlier I had set big goals for the New Year.

This was before I became gritty and committed to performance psychology full time, and I'd spent the prior year running in races across the country and starting to finish in the top ten out of thousands of race participants. So this year, I was determined to train harder, eat better, and finish in the top three.

I had read all of the stories about Kobe Bryant, Joe De Sena, Tim Grover, and countless other successes, and I used their guidance to set my plan for the year. It was going to be simple. I was going to help my modern brain and ignore my primitive brain. I was going to use my want power and focus my attention on getting small wins. But when I woke up in a city so cold that it was being called "Chiberia," I lost my motivation.

My head was filled with all of the completely rational reasons why I should skip my training, set my alarm for later, and head right back to sleep.

It's dangerous to run in this type of weather.
I can't run inside because the treadmill might give me shin splints.
What is one day going to matter?
Sleep is good for your muscles.
I have been training so hard recently, I deserve to have one day where I rest.

You have probably thought of similar excuses at some point in your life. But what you might not realize is how important these crossroad moments are to reaching your goals. This is the time that you make the decision about how committed you really are to achieving what you want. This is the middle of the journey—and it is by far the hardest part.

It is easy to find motivation on December 31 when you are visualizing what life will be like when you accomplish your goal. You see your results, you see your progress, and you get excited about your plan to get there. It is also easy to find motivation when you are nearing the completion of your goal. You see what you have been able to accomplish, and you are confident that you will be able to see it through to the end. You may even work harder as you realize how close you are to the finish line.

In order to get there, however, you need to make it through the middle, when the motivation from setting your goals has worn off, and the end is weeks, months, or even years away. That is when one day of progress seems completely insignificant in comparison with the higher goal. That is when your willpower is really tested. That is when the true achievers set themselves apart from the rest of the pack. Only 8 percent of people are able to push through the temptation to quit. The other 92 percent of people get lost in the middle of the journey.

They wake up tired, they wake up to cold weather, they wake up and "do not feel right," so they take the day off. Then that day sets the precedent that it is okay to take another day off. Then before they know it, they have given up entirely.

You can see how excited J.K. Rowling was about Harry Potter when she first came up with the idea. She wanted to write everything down as fast as she could put pen to paper. And at some point in writing her book, she hit the place where she was so close to the finish that it didn't make any sense to give up. The hardest days for her were in the middle, when she woke up as an unemployed single mother and there was no end in sight. And she didn't just have to deal with those days for weeks or months. She had to deal with them for years.

Getting through the Middle

The rest of this chapter will give you the tools to join the 8 percent of people like Rowling who are able to make it through the middle of their journeys, to do the hard, sometimes monotonous, work on a consistent basis that it takes to accomplish big things. If you can heed the lessons of this chapter, you will begin to enjoy the challenge of getting through the middle of the journey, and count yourself among those select few who make it to the finish. These are some strategies for getting through the middle:

1) *Win the day.* There is perhaps no harder "middle of the journey" than the one in getting over an addiction to drugs or alcohol. At that point, addicts have lost their initial enthusiasm for quitting and the process has become extremely painful. They have yet to create their new sober lifestyles, and the temptation to slip back to their usual vices is at its highest point.

    So what do Alcoholics Anonymous (AA) and many other substance abuse treatment programs do to help their patients get through these excruciating times? They have one simple rule: "Do not have a drink *today*."

    They know that if their patients focus on a huge goal, like giving up alcohol for months, years, or the rest of their lives, the task will seem impossible. But by breaking it down to just making it through the day, the addict has a simple goal that is realistic and attainable. This builds his confidence as he achieves his goal every day. Before long, it has been a week, a month, or even a year since he last used—and he is feeling more confident than ever that he *can* do this.

    When you set goals, you probably focus on the results. You see the "after" photo of your life and get excited to make it reality. But when you hit the middle of the journey, each day becomes a constant reminder of just how far you are from achieving that result.

    If you shift your focus to simply winning the day, however, your confidence will grow with each day. You will not get bogged down by how far you are from achieving your ultimate goal. Instead, your goal becomes realistic and attainable. You see the value in the progress you make each day, rather than feeling it was insignificant.

Use the "after" photo to guide where you want to go, but then focus all your attention on what you need to do *each day* to get there. Forget about the result, and focus your attention on the process.

2) *Monitor your progress.* After master of comedy Jerry Seinfeld finished one of his live performances, a young comedian came to his dressing room and asked him, "What is your secret to success?"

   Seinfeld turned to the young man and said, "In order to succeed at comedy, you need to tell better jokes. And in order to tell better jokes, you need to write every day. So what you need to do is get a giant calendar of the whole year, and every day that you write a new joke, mark a big red X on that day. Then it is as simple as not breaking the chain."

   That's it. That's what moved Seinfeld from your typical struggling comic to a place where he's *still* pulling in a cool eighty million dollars a year. He monitored his progress in a concrete, visible way, so he could see how each day moved him closer to his goal. This is a natural extension of "winning the day," but it is just as important. Marking each day that you achieved your goal with a big red X builds confidence. It is the proof that you have won the day.

   As you continue to achieve your goal each day, you see the giant chain being made and you gain extra motivation not to break it. The Seinfeld method increases your level of self-awareness and makes winning the day something measurable and concrete. When you use it to monitor yourself, you will see that the motivation to not break the chain is powerful. It may just give you that extra edge you need to win the day!

3) *Understand that it will get easier.* The middle of the journey is like the second act of a great movie, when the protagonist faces an extraordinarily hard challenge and her character is tested. She must overcome this huge level of adversity to achieve her happy ending in the third act.

You may face a time when the challenges in the middle of the journey feel like they will last forever. You may feel so tired or demoralized by how far away you are from achieving your goal that you will be tempted to give up.

You must understand that such moments do not last forever. These moments are the ones that test how much you really want something. If you can fight through them, taking it day by day, things will get easier. You will adapt to the necessary changes in your behavior and develop habits that make it easier to engage in daily deliberate practice. You will focus on each day as its own success, you will see a huge chain of red X's on your calendar, and you will begin to feel and act more like your ideal self. And with each day, you will become more confident in the process.

The Myth of the Big Idea

There are few ideas that explode in the way that Harry Potter did. J.K. Rowling would have been considered insane if she predicted that her children's novel about a boy going to a school for magic would turn her into a billionaire. But it did. The idea was brilliant.

Rowling's idea for Harry Potter is one of many that lead us to believe that greatness is simply a result of the "big idea." We hear about the stories of massive success like Henry Ford creating the assembly line, Bill Gates envisioning a world with a computer on every desk, and Mark Zuckerberg stealing the massively successful idea for Facebook. We then believe that in order to achieve greatness in our own right we must come up with our own big idea.

But as we have learned through Rowling's story, the big idea is simply the starting point. It is certainly important—Rowling wouldn't have captivated the world with a boring story—but far more important is what comes after the idea. Rowling became a hugely successful author because of everything that took place after the train ride. If she did not have the passion, the willpower, and the grit to fight through all of her hardships, her big idea would have been irrelevant. Do not be seduced by the big idea. An idea is important, but far more important is the will to do whatever it takes to turn that idea into reality.

Conclusion

Success is 1 percent inspiration and 99 percent perspiration. J.K. Rowling fully admits that she was lucky to come up with the idea for Harry Potter while she was riding that train from Manchester to London. However, enduring five years of poverty, depression, and a constant battle with her realistic self to keep writing certainly was not luck. That was passion and perseverance toward a long-term goal. That was grit.

Grit is not the same as willpower. You can have willpower and pursue many different goals at the same time, which may lead you to relative success, but it will not lead you to the greatness achieved by the heroes in this book. To achieve greatness, you must focus your willpower on one specific long-term goal, fight through the middle of the journey, and see it through to completion.

Key Points

- *Grit is one of the greatest indicators of success.* Those who achieve greatness aren't always the smartest, richest, or most talented. Instead, they have the highest levels of passion and perseverance. They are gritty.

- *Grit is different than willpower.* Unlike willpower, grit is focused on one very specific goal. J.K. Rowling wasn't writing a book while also trying to cure cancer. She was focused solely on getting Harry onto bookshelves.

- *The middle of the journey is the hardest.* It's easy to find motivation when you're just getting started, and it's easy to find motivation when you can see the finish line. Where most people fail is in the middle, when the initial enthusiasm wears off and the end seems so far away.

- *Get through the middle day by day.* The best way to get through the middle is to focus on simply making progress each day. This will help you build confidence, achieve small wins, and eventually see the finish line.

- *Great ideas don't create greatness.* J.K. Rowling had a billion-dollar idea on her train ride. But the idea itself isn't why Harry Potter became an international icon. It was because she had the willpower to persevere through five years of hard times.

Strategies

1) *Assess your grit.* Are you focusing your willpower on one thing? If not, is there one thing you care about more than all others? Assess your goals and priorities to see if you can be grittier.

2) *Come up with a specific, measurable goal to achieve each day.* Find one thing to be your daily win. It will be really easy to cheat, so make sure the goal is specific and measurable.

3) *Mark your daily wins.* Get a calendar that you will see several times a day, and begin marking your daily wins with a big X. Do not cheat!

Chapter 7

Opening Your Mind

"Stay hungry, stay foolish."
– Steve Jobs

Steve Jobs could not believe his eyes as he looked at the computer screen. It was one of the most significant moments in computing history. His best friend, Steve Wozniak, had built a machine that combined keyboard, screen, and computer into a single unit that fit on a desktop. For the first time, someone could press a key and have the corresponding letter show up on a computer screen. Jobs was blown away by the possibilities he saw in front of him.

Could the computer be networked? Was it possible to add discs for memory storage? How much would people pay for the first real personal computer?

Wozniak's simple goal for the computer was to give it away for free to his friends and fellow engineers at the Homebrew Computer Club. But Jobs knew that the machine was far too important to give away for free. In that box, he saw an opportunity. He recognized the technological revolution that was taking place all around him, and he knew that, with that machine, he could create a company that would lead the way. So he convinced Wozniak to become his business partner, and the two created Apple Computer.

Wozniak and Jobs got right to work on the new company, Wozniak putting the finishing touches on the "Apple I" (as they named the machine) and Jobs going out to find people to buy it. Sure enough, Jobs was right about people being willing to buy the Apple I. He sold an order of fifty computers to a small store in Palo Alto—despite the fact that Apple Computer did not have the parts, labor, or capital to actually produce the order. But that was irrelevant to Jobs. He convinced friends to work for him, he convinced dealers to sell their parts on credit, and he convinced Wozniak to spend hours of time after his day job to produce Apple's first order.

After successfully filling that order, Jobs knew he was on to something—and he also knew that he needed some capital to grow his company. He spent hours every day on the phone in his parents' kitchen, talking to potential investors. Over and over, he was rejected. He was asking for far too much capital for far too little equity, in a far too risky business. But Jobs was not fazed. He knew what was possible.

After receiving countless rejections, Jobs finally convinced Mike Markkula, an investor who'd capitalized on the huge success of his former company Intel, to buy a 33 percent equity stake in Apple Computer for $250,000. With Markkula's capital, the company was able to create the computer that would cement their status among the top computer companies in Silicon Valley: the Apple II.

The Reality Distortion Field

As Apple Computer began to grow at a rapid rate, Jobs stepped aside from the CEO position to let someone with more experience take over. He was in his early twenties and understood he was not ready for the job. Instead, he took a role as the product manager for a new premium computer he would call the "Lisa."

On the Lisa team, his peculiar and disruptive style as a manager was put on display. He wanted absolutely every detail of the Lisa to be perfect. He obsessed over quality and berated members of his team for giving him "shit work." Eventually, this obsession with perfection made the Lisa far too expensive, and Jobs was sent to work on a new project, the lower-cost Macintosh.

When he joined the Macintosh team, he put on full display that which was both his biggest asset and his biggest flaw: his reality distortion field. "Reality distortion field" was a term coined by the Macintosh team to describe Jobs' complete disregard for the rules of reality. To Jobs, everything in his mind was not only possible, but was already reality. He would tell his engineers to get something done in half the time the task required. His visions of the future sounded completely insane to his team. But once they began working on his crazy ideas, they started to become real.

"You did the impossible because you didn't realize it was impossible!" remembered Debby Coleman, one of the members of the Macintosh team. She was one of many engineers who were inspired by Jobs to question the rules of what they knew about the world of computing.

Jobs' reality distortion field originated in his belief that the rules didn't apply to him. That's why he dropped out of college, that's why he dropped acid, and that's why he dropped his great job at Atari to start Apple Computer in the first place. He was going to create the world based on his rules, not let the world's rules create him. His refusal to accept limits is best summed up by what happened when Jobs was prototyping the Mac. He was frustrated by how long it took to start up, so he asked his engineer, "If making the Mac start up ten seconds faster would save someone's life, could you do it?" The engineer then proceeded to think outside the box and make it start up *twenty-seven* seconds faster.

Jobs' reality distortion field did have a downside, however. Jobs constantly lied, bent the truth, stole ideas from members of his team that he originally said were "shit," and refused to believe that which he did not want to be true. The worst example was in the birth of his first daughter, Lisa Brennan. Even after taking a paternity test that proved with 96 percent accuracy that he was the father, Jobs continued to deny that Lisa was his child. He simply did not want to believe it. Unfortunately for Jobs, his arrogance, deception, and denial of anything that didn't fit his idea of reality overpowered the benefits of his reality distortion field, ultimately leading to Apple Computer's board of directors voting him out of the company in 1985.

Seeing the World Differently

Steve Jobs was flawed. He was arrogant, ruthless, and cold to many of the people in his life. But he acted this way for the same reason that he was able to be a revolutionary innovator and change the world for the rest of us: He believed that the rules did not apply to him. The rules about computers simply being efficient business machines didn't apply. The rules about what an engineer on his team could and couldn't do didn't apply. And later, the rules about taking a seemingly hopeless company and making it the greatest in the world didn't apply.

What would happen to your willpower if you started bending your idea of reality as Jobs did? The answer lies in the story of Daniel Everett, a missionary sent deep into the heart of the Amazon jungle to teach Christianity to a tribe known as the Piraha.

The Piraha language has been called the hardest on the planet. It seems to have no grammar structure, no alphabet, and no past or future tense. Previous missionaries had spent years trying to understand the language, but they were nearly driven insane trying to communicate with the tribe. Everett, however, was confident. He believed that with his advanced degree in linguistics and enough perseverance, he would be able to meet the challenge and be the first to crack the code.

When he arrived, he immediately started making great progress. He spent a full year in the village with the tribe, learning more every day. He took copious notes on each word and learned much of the vocabulary. But one day he stopped making progress. Some things just didn't make sense. They didn't have a word for left or right. They had multiple meanings for certain words that didn't seem to connect. With each step forward, Everett felt as if he was taking two steps back.

This must have been when the previous missionaries went insane, he thought. Clearly, learning this language was not impossible. Children in the tribe seemed to pick it up with ease. So why couldn't he?

After months of feeling like he was getting nowhere, Everett finally ventured outside the village. He joined the Piraha men on one of their hunts and discovered something remarkable. The language they used while hunting was completely different than the language used in the village. They communicated with different pitches of whistling that allowed them to be stealthier when stalking their prey. This was a completely foreign idea to Everett. Nothing he'd learned in school had prepared him for a people who used completely different languages in different scenarios. It was then that it hit him: He had been looking at the Piraha language in the wrong way.

Everett realized that he had been trying to learn how the Piraha language fit into his idea of how language is structured, with specific vocabulary, grammar, an alphabet, and so on—when in fact, the Piraha language did not fit into any such structures. The reason that the tribe's children were able to learn the language easily is because they had no prior concept of linguistic structure. They weren't trying to fit a square peg in a round hole; they simply observed and learned with a completely open mind.

This is why Jobs' reality distortion field was so effective. To him, there were no rules. There was no "round hole" that you had to fit the rules of engineering and computing into. There were only endless possibilities.

And that is what he instilled in his team. He was able to get them to stop thinking like Daniel Everett and to start thinking like the Piraha children. He was able to shift them into what author Robert Greene calls a "dimensional mind."

The Dimensional Mind

In his book *Mastery,* Greene argues that we all start life with this same open mind. Everything we see is new and exciting to us. We seek to learn about things without placing judgment on them. We don't see our culture or way of life as better or worse than others. We simply learn and observe, accepting our role as the student.

As we grow older, though, we start closing our minds. We start realizing what is "realistic." We start building a world of rules, the same way Daniel Everett did with language.

He saw himself as the intelligent scientist coming to study the Piraha language the same way he might study a textbook. As a result, he didn't fully embrace their culture and couldn't see its powerful connection to their language. Once he let go of this need to adhere to the rules of language, however, he learned the Piraha language with ease.

A shift like Everett's change in his mental perspective creates a "dimensional mind." The dimensional mind is open. It holds no judgment regarding what is and isn't possible. Like a child, it simply observes and learns.

Cultivating a dimensional mind helps you overcome one of the biggest stumbling blocks on the road to greatness: the feeling that your rules are correct. It allows you to be truly curious. It keeps you from subconsciously placing judgments on things before you start to explore the details.

The key is to never be satisfied with what you have learned, which is not natural for us as humans. Your brain wants to genuinely believe that it knows everything that it needs to know about the world around you, a tactic used by your primitive brain to help you conserve mental energy. To avoid this, you need to understand that no matter what you know today, there is always more to learn. With this perspective, you can begin to implement the techniques below that will open your mind and help you learn.

Cultivating a Dimensional Mind

Make no mistake about it, opening up your mind to new ideas is not easy. But the pain of admitting that you may be wrong and changing your beliefs will never be as great as the pain of sticking your head in the sand—wasting weeks, months, or years continuing down the wrong path. Although it will be a lifelong struggle to cultivate a truly dimensional mind, there are several proven tactics that you can use to train your mind to become more open:

1) *Practice curiosity.* You probably take so many things in your world for granted. You see a kitchen table as just a kitchen table, a computer as just a computer, and a car as just a car. But where did they all come from? How do they all work? When you were child, you asked questions like that. You were curious about everything around you, and that trained your brain to open.

   As you know, the brain works like a muscle. If you exercise your curiosity about one thing, it will begin to become more curious about everything else. So take ten to fifteen minutes every day to simply be more curious about the world around you. Look at people, objects, and technology, and wonder, "Why? How?" You don't even need to find the answers. You just need to open your mind to the questions.

2) *Detach your ego from your ideas.* We have a natural tendency to attach ourselves to our ideas. We believe that they represent our character, intelligence, and values—so when our ideas are challenged, we feel as if it is our character being challenged.

   In order to cultivate a dimensional mind, you must learn to detach yourself from this notion. Ten years ago, you may have not have held the same ideas that you do now. Would you consider yourself ten years ago as less of a person of character because of that? Of course not. You simply had less experience and a different perspective than you do today.

You must be open to learning, growing, and constantly changing your ideas and beliefs. The only way you can do this is by recognizing that your current ideas do not define who you are. They are merely your best understanding of your world at the current time. If you can learn to detach your ego from your beliefs, you will be much more open to new and better ideas that come across your path.

3) *Let go of your need to judge.* We all have an ideal world that is based on our own belief system. When you spend time observing others' behavior, you judge everything you see against your own ideal of how you believe things should be. Every time you do this, you are training your brain to become more closed off to new ideas. You are reinforcing your current belief system and not allowing yourself to see another person's perspective.

   To overcome this tendency, you must identify the situations where you begin to judge others. When you recognize such situations, you can make a conscious effort to see things from the other person's point of view. This trains your mind to become more open to new ideas, perspectives, and beliefs.

4) *Seek out the unfamiliar.* When it comes to belief systems, we have a horrible tendency to have an "us versus them" mentality. Whether about religion, politics, or life values, we despise opposing arguments so much that we generally do not seek to understand them. We approach them with a closed mind, looking for the flaws in their logic. The more you engage in this practice, however, the more you will close yourself off to other unfamiliar ideas. If you train your mind to be closed in matters of politics, you will also be more set in your beliefs about relationships, science, and religion.

Avoid this trap by seeking out unfamiliar knowledge with an open mind. Read books written by those with different ideas than you. Tune in to a news station known to hold opposing political views from yours. Simply by being open to learning, you will train your brain to become more open to all new ideas.

5) *Be more mindful of your decisions.* What you decide to eat, what you decide to wear, and what you decide to do when you first get to work are all decisions made by your brain on autopilot. These automatic choices are made by the same part of your brain that wants to tune out opposing ideas. By consistently running on autopilot, you are essentially being closed-minded in your daily decision-making, training your brain to become closed-minded in its higher thinking as well.

You can overcome this tendency by becoming more mindful of your daily decisions. This is as simple as pausing to question why you are getting coffee as soon as you make it into the office or why you are eating cereal for breakfast rather than eggs. Questioning these daily decisions will train your mind to be more open to other ideas as well. You do not need to change your behavior; you just need to question it.

The Need for Discipline

After the ousting of Steve Jobs in 1985, Apple suffered a slow march toward what seemed like its death. Over the next decade, the company languished without any groundbreaking products. Rather than focusing on doing one thing and doing it extremely well, they spread themselves too thin. They started with computers for the average person. Then they decided to add some computers for business. Then they added premium computers. Then they decided to get into the personal digital assistant market with their

"Newton." None of these were bad ideas, per se, but by trying to do more and more things, they didn't do *anything* particularly well.

None of Apple's three different CEOs during that time were able to provide a clear direction for the company. It was so bad, in fact, that in 1997 when Michael Dell—founder of the Dell computer company—was asked what he would do if he were the head of Apple, he said, "What would I do? I'd shut it down and give the money back to the shareholders."

Apple seemed to have lost all hope and was seriously considering selling off its assets. There seemed no realistic chance of restoring the company to its former greatness. So, the board of directors decided to take a huge gamble and bring back the man who didn't care about what was realistic. They offered Jobs his former position as head of the company.

Even Jobs' reality distortion field, however, wasn't enough to blind him from the truth about Apple. Things were so bad when he took over that he told the press, "Apple is like a ship with a hole in the bottom, leaking water. And my job is to get the ship pointed in the right direction."

In his time away from Apple, Jobs had matured. He no longer wanted to do everything, and do it all perfectly. He understood that the company and its products could not be all things to all people. So instead of chasing any and all opportunities in business, music, and personal digital assistants—as the company had been doing since his departure—he brought the company back to what made them great in the first place: the Macintosh personal computer. Everything that didn't have to do with making the Macintosh the best computer in the marketplace was cut. Before envisioning any of the extraordinary and world-changing products that Apple would create over the next fifteen years, Apple had to first get back to basics and win the battle that they were already in. And as a result, they slowly but surely began to dominate the personal computer world.

When they won that battle, Jobs led Apple to explore a new music-playing device they would call the "iPod," which, in Jobs' mind, was merely "an important and natural extension of the Macintosh." Apple believed the iPod would simply extend the value of the Mac by allowing users to take the music stored on their Mac with them. Suddenly, Apple was dominating the MP3-player market, which helped Jobs realize that they could move into actual sales of music online. With millions of customers already in possession of iPods, the company had leverage to dominate that market as well.

Product by product and market by market, Apple won battle after battle. A mere thirteen years after Michael Dell said that they should shut the company down, Apple had evolved into the most valuable company in the world, proving that a reality distortion field can be stretched beyond building a single revolutionary product.

Blending the Dimensional Mind and Discipline

As important as it was for Jobs to cultivate a dimensional mindset, this alone was not enough for him to make his greatest contributions to the computing world. As Jim Collins pointed out in his book *Great by Choice,* when Jobs returned as the CEO of Apple, he did not just bring innovation back to the company; he brought discipline.

Instead of following his predecessors by chasing irrelevant opportunities, he focused on only one thing and doing that thing to perfection. He could have continued building business computers, personal digital assistants, and premium computers with the "Steve Jobs creative touch," but he didn't. He knew the value of creativity, but he also knew the value of discipline.

Most of us go about achieving our goals the same way that Apple did before Jobs' return. We want to start eating healthy, exercising regularly, improving our productivity, and making more time for important things like family, all at once—which, of course, leads us to become completely overwhelmed. Rather than doing any one of those things well, we end up doing them all poorly, and stressing ourselves out in the process. As you know, your willpower is like a muscle. If you use it for one goal, you will tire it out for the next one, which means the more things you add to your list, the less effective you will be at any of them.

You must be disciplined about finishing what you have started before you move on to another goal. New goals may be sexy—they certainly seem that way compared to the discipline that it takes to finish your current goal—but those new goals will seem just as boring and uninteresting once your initial enthusiasm has worn off and the finish line still seems so far away. Starting on another goal before you've achieved your first will only land you with a pile of half-finished goals and few results to show for them.

The next time you become tempted by the lure of a new and exciting goal, pause. Think about your current goals and ambitions. Remember that what you're working on right now once seemed just as exciting. This self-awareness will help you realize what this newer and more exciting project really is: just a distraction. Crossing the finish line of your current goal will always be more rewarding than making it halfway to the finish of a new one, so summon the discipline and willpower to win the battle you are already in.

Conclusion

Steve Jobs is a fascinating figure. He was both an inspiration and an asshole. He was both a genius and a fool. And he was both dimensional-minded and disciplined. He was at the front of the technology revolution because he saw the world differently. He felt that the rules of science, engineering, and even common sense did not apply to him. With his disregard of reality, he was able to create some of the most amazing products for sale today.

However, his dimensional mind alone was not what led to Jobs' greatest impact on the world. When Jobs returned to the company he founded, he didn't just bring his open-mindedness; he brought discipline. He brought the company back to basics, ensuring that they won the battle they were already in before expanding further. Then, with his combination of open-mindedness and discipline, he led Apple from hopelessness to greatness.

To achieve the same level of success as Steve Jobs, you must fight against your tendency to judge things as "realistic" or "impossible." You must train your mind to be open and never be satisfied with what you have learned. Then you must summon the discipline to focus your newfound dimensional mind on one thing at a time. In this way, you will find yourself winning goal after goal, battle after battle, until you achieve whatever greatness you seek.

Key Points

- *Your brain has a set of rules.* You created these rules to help you make sense of the world, but they are hardly scientific facts. Steve Jobs succeeded because he helped people open their minds to what could be, rather than what was.

- *You can break these rules by cultivating a dimensional mind.* A dimensional mind sees the world without judgment or a sense of limits. Like the mind of a child, it simply observes and learns. Being curious, nonjudgmental, and open to new ideas will train your brain to become more dimensional.

- *Greatness requires a disciplined dimensional mind.* Jobs made his greatest contribution to the world when he blended his creativity with the discipline of accomplishing one goal at a time. In the same way, your creativity will be much more effective when it is focused on one goal at a time.

Strategies

1) *Practice curiosity.* Begin a daily practice of questioning the world around you. Simply take ten minutes to ponder things you usually take for granted.

2) *Detach your ego from your ideas.* Your current ideas are a reflection of your understanding, not your character. Being wrong is a part of learning and growing.

3) *Become mindful of your judgments.* Being judgmental will train your mind to be closed. When you're tempted to judge someone, think honestly about whether your judgment will benefit anything—is it worth stifling your creativity?

4) *Learn about something unfamiliar.* Read, watch, or experience something you're unfamiliar with. As you do so, ensure that your goal is learning, not confirming your own biases.

5) *Win the battle you are in.* Focus all of your creativity on one thing at a time. Finish what you started before you move on to something new.

Chapter 8

Overcoming Limits

"Pain doesn't exist for me. I know it is there, but I don't pay attention to it."
– Jure Robic

It has been called the hardest competition on the planet. The Insight Race Across America is a 3,000-mile nonstop bike race from one end of the United States to the other—more than 36 percent longer than the Tour de France. But as the competing cyclists made their final preparations for the 2005 race, their fear was not the pain they would face over the full week of biking. Their fear was of the seemingly inhuman winner of the 2004 race, Jure Robic.

Since the race is nonstop, each rider chooses exactly how long he rests, how much he eats, and how long he sleeps. He must bike as fast as he can, for as long as he can, while also sleeping as little as he can. This means that it is just as important to be mentally strong as it is to be physically strong—and that is exactly where Robic beat out his twenty-three competitors.

First, he faced the heat of the desert, riding in temperatures over 100 degrees Fahrenheit. During those miles, he did not just have to deal with the discomfort of the heat, but he was also at such risk of dehydration that he needed to drink as much as one liter of water per hour.

After the heat, Robic's digestive tract was tested. He had to consume more than 10,000 calories every day, which is more than the body is comfortable with and leads to issues like severe nausea and diarrhea—which, of course, are made worse by constant movement and physical exertion.

Next came the problems with the points of contact between Robic's body and the bike. His feet swelled to about double their normal size. His thumb nerves stopped functioning properly. And when he was later asked about the contact between his rear end and the seat itself...he didn't want to talk about it.

So how do the typical twenty-four racers endure this tprture for seven to ten days? Better yet, how did Robic endure this kind of pain while biking faster than every other rider and only sleeping ninety minutes per night? Robic was able to accomplish this extraordinary feat of willpower because he did not give himself any choices.

To endure this hardship, Robic only gave himself a choice over his music, food, and bathroom breaks. He left every other decision up to his support crew. They decided when he rested, they decided when he ate, and they decided how fast he must go. "We are Jure's software," said Miran Stanovnik, a member of Robic's support crew. "He is the hardware going down the road. It is best if he has no idea about these things. He rides—that is all." And ride he did. Without making any critical decisions, Jure Robic rode to world-record finishes over and over again.

But how does this system work? It seems to make no sense. Who better to know when Robic needed to rest than Robic himself? Also, weren't there limits to how fast he could go? Why would he leave a decision like that up to a support crew who had no idea how his muscles felt? To answer these questions, let's look at what was happening in Robic's body as he worked himself to exhaustion.

Fatigue

For centuries, physiologists believed that we feel exhaustion when we physically cannot go any further. Fatigue, they thought, is what occurs when the muscles in our bodies cannot do any more work until they replenish their energy. While this made sense in theory, they could never scientifically prove that was what actually made exercisers give up.

There was one physiologist, however, who did not believe in that fatigue theory. In 1924, Archibald Hill proposed the idea that when the body is depleting its energy, the brain will send messages in the form of pain to the muscles.

Hill believed that the brain does this to conserve energy to survive the many hardships early humans dealt with. He theorized that the brain makes it *feel* as if our muscles are incapable of working in order to motivate us to rest and recover, but that we actually have plenty of energy remaining. Unfortunately, Hill lacked the technology to prove his theory, so it fell upon deaf ears.

Fifty years later, however, an ultramarathoner and sports scientist named Timothy Noakes began testing Hill's theory. He found that the brain of an athlete was indeed sending messages to the body to stop when it sensed rapidly depleting energy stores. These messages from the brain are what we call "fatigue."

Noakes' conclusion, then, was that even in times when it feels as if you are out of energy, you really have plenty at your disposal. This discovery proved that fatigue is not a physiological phenomenon; it is actually more of an emotion. Just like the emotion anxiety motivates us to hold back from giving a public speech, fatigue motivates us to hold back from reaching our true physical limitations. In both cases, these emotions are our brains' way of trying to keep us safe from perceived pain.

So, whether they knew it or not, Robic and his crew had actually cracked the scientific code to beating fatigue. Because he ignored his own brain's messages and listened only to his crew, he conditioned himself to ignore his sense of fatigue. Over time, Robic's crew saw that he could push himself far beyond his initial feeling of fatigue. When Robic said that he could not possibly push any more, his crew knew they could motivate him to keep going.

The Limits of Willpower

Is it possible that this same phenomenon is true of our willpower muscle? Could your brain make you feel as if you were completely out of willpower, when really you could keep pushing like Robic?

To answer this question, let's go back once more to our ancestors. As you probably recall, your primitive brain is wired for survival. It will motivate you to eat, to stay safe from potential dangers, and in the case of Robic, to stop cycling and rest.

This part of your brain still believes that you are living in the Stone Age. It does not know where your next meal is coming from or whether you're going to need to escape a lion lurking around the corner, so your primitive brain sends messages instructing you to rest and refuel as soon as you get low on energy. That way, it reasons, you will have enough left to survive in case you can't find food or you need to make a daring escape.

This primitive part of your brain is a powerful motivator, but it does not call the shots. You also have your modern brain that allows you to think, plan, and exert willpower. This part of your brain is the final decision-maker. It has the ability to override the primitive brain's instructions to stop and rest. It has the power to endure pain and keep you going through a challenge.

This does not, however, mean that overriding your primitive emotions is easy. The lower you get on energy, the harder it is to access your willpower and ignore your impulses to indulge, procrastinate, and get off the treadmill.

But imagine you are back in the Stone Age. You are in the same position as Robic and feel like you have no energy left. Your brain is motivating you to rest and replenish. But then you see a gazelle in the distance. You need to hunt down this potential meal! When this happens, your brain immediately stops sending you messages to rest. Instead, it accesses your want power and gives you the energy and motivation that you need to successfully hunt down that gazelle. Your brain will tap into whatever energy you have left if it believes that doing so is worth it.

This is where your want power truly shines. Even if you feel completely drained of willpower, you still have the ultimate ability to say "no" to dessert. Even if all you want to do is lay on your couch and watch TV, you can still force yourself to clean your kitchen. Even if you feel like your eyes are crossing from staring at books so long, you can still force yourself to keep studying. There may be a final limit to what you are able to will yourself to do, but that limit is far beyond your first feelings of exhaustion.

The Comfort Zone

Sometimes, though, limits you face have nothing to do with what you are able to accomplish physically, or even mentally. The biggest limits are your own perceptions of what you are incapable of achieving—the knowledge that certain things lie outside of your comfort zone.

You probably do not fear failure as much as you fear being perceived as a failure. That is why venturing outside of your comfort zone is so scary. In doing so, you feel that you are setting yourself up for criticism, ridicule, and embarrassment. Unfortunately, one of the places that this happens most is at the gym. Many newcomers simply do not know the proper exercises, the proper weights, or the proper form, and they are self-conscious about it. The thought of looking stupid while exercising in front of others is one of the reasons that many people aren't able to regularly exercise.

A young man, whom I'll call Brent, went through this experience. He was a tall, lanky nineteen-year-old who worked out on occasion but didn't know how to properly lift weights. He usually went to the gym with a friend because he was never confident enough to go by himself. But one day his friend couldn't make it, and Brent realized that if he was going to reach his goals, he was going to have to face his fears and start working out on his own.

So he went to the gym by himself—and it was a disaster. He was nervous from the moment he pushed through the gym doors. He started off with squats—quite possibly the hardest lift there is—and things did not go well. On his fourth of five sets, Brent's knees buckled and he fell. A couple of people in the gym started to laugh, which according to him hurt far worse than the fall. But he got back up, took a little bit of weight off, and finished his last set.

Now he was understandably feeling even more nervous than when he'd arrived. He could feel the stares of those around him as he approached the next exercise, deadlift. He'd never really gotten the form down when exercising with his friend, and his knees were feeling weak from the nerves and the squats.

On his first set, he started with a very low weight, but his knees still could not take the pressure. Brent fell once more and, because of the loud noise, it felt like the whole gym was staring at him. Feeling completely embarrassed at this point, Brent couldn't take it any longer. He left the gym feeling like a disgrace.

You cannot help but feel bad for Brent. Here is someone willing to be vulnerable in order to improve himself, yet he faced ridicule that was just too much. There was probably little chance that he would be able to gain the courage to go back to the gym after something that embarrassing—that is, until Arnold Schwarzenegger saw his story. Arnold wrote Brent this message:

Someone told me about this. I hope I'm not too late here, I'm traveling, but I wanted to chime in. I always say don't be afraid of failure, because how far can you really fall? You found out—to the ground. It's right there. Now you know it isn't anything that should scare you. You should be proud that you weren't afraid—not embarrassed that you failed. You could have made excuses not to walk in the door, but you didn't.

You knew it would be hard, and it would be uncomfortable, and it might be awkward—and you did it anyway. That's courage. I'm proud of you.

The last guy I rooted for broke a world record in the deadlift. You have more in common with him than you think.

First, he started out lifting just the bar, too (when you look at him, he may have been three months old at that point). Second, imagine his courage. He walked up to that bar in front of a big audience and television cameras, knowing that not only had he never lifted that much before—NO ONE on earth had—and it was highly likely he would completely fail. You may not think about it this way, but you showed that courage, on a smaller level. Finally, I'm rooting for you, too. You took the first step and you fell, but at least you fell in the right direction, so get back up and take the next step. Keep moving forward.

The limits that you perceive in your mind are made worse by the fear of failure, a fear that, as Arnold put it, is unfounded. Brent went through about as terrible of an experience as he could, but what were the consequences, really? He still did five sets of squats and a set of deadlifts that he wouldn't have done had he sat at home in fear of what might have happened. And he may have fallen, but he only hit the ground. The next day, those people who laughed had forgotten about him. And he was one day stronger because he went to the gym and tried.

Why We Fear Being Vulnerable

We have a natural desire to be admired by people, so we fear exposing our weaknesses to them. Millions of years ago, exposing our weaknesses could have meant the difference between life and death. Venturing outside of safety and comfort exposed us to predators, and it showed our weaknesses to other tribe members, which could mean banishment and almost-certain death. So we wanted to hide our weaknesses and ensure that we were liked and respected by the tribe.

Fast-forward to the present day, where being vulnerable usually isn't a matter of life and death. As Arnold asked in his response to Brent, "How far can you really fall?" For Brent, it was to the ground. That was it. He didn't die. He didn't lose any friends. And he actually gained respect from one of the most successful people alive.

You probably build up situations to be much bigger in your head than they actually are. Brent left the gym feeling completely low. He felt as if he could never become a regular exerciser and that everybody in the gym was going to make fun of him if he ever came back. But would any gym member even remember him? Would they even care? Would it even matter if they did?

Life outside of your comfort zone looks scary. And sometimes venturing outside of it actually *is* scary. But the more you venture outside of it and make yourself vulnerable, the more comfortable you will become. You will learn that making mistakes is not the end of the world—and that the real embarrassment is not having the courage to even try.

Leaving Your Comfort Zone

As with everything you have learned in this book, knowing that your fear of life outside of your comfort zone is unfounded is only half the battle. Just because your fear comes from a part of your brain that was developed millions of years ago does not mean you can just wish that fear away. It's there. And it will always be there.

However, as Nelson Mandela once said, "Courage is not the absence of fear, but the triumph over it." Here are some proven ways to help you triumph over any fears of vulnerability as you leave your comfort zone:

1) *Let go of your judgments.* For better or worse, you probably judge people you see on their attractiveness, their communication skills, or their intelligence. Every time you do this, you train your brain to believe everyone else is also judging you. Because you spend your time judging others against an ideal, you become afraid that you, too, will not live up to your own high standards.

   To overcome this tendency, you must train your mind to let go of judgment. When you recognize that you are judging others, especially based on performance, stop. Think about whether being judgmental is helping anything, or if it is just feeding your ego. Then try to allow yourself to see things from the other person's perspective. This trains your mind to become more open to learning and making mistakes, helping you become more comfortable being vulnerable.

2) *Stay in the present.* Almost all of your fear of being vulnerable takes place in the future. You envision venturing outside of your comfort zone, you see yourself failing, and you feel the embarrassment that your future self will go through. This fear puts an extraordinary layer of stress and anxiety on you for no reason. Your future failure may not actually happen, and even if it does, you probably envision the consequences being much worse than they actually will be.

   Instead, train your brain to stay in the present. There is no unnecessary suffering in the present. You don't foresee future failure, and you don't rehash past embarrassing moments. You simply deal with whatever situation is in front of you.

   This is where our old friend meditation comes in. Meditation will train your brain to let go of fears of the future and regrets of the past. It will help you stay focused on the present and embrace vulnerable situations.

3) *Shift your perspective.* Shifting your perspective will help you tap into your want power as you begin to forget about your trivial fears and see the big picture instead. To shift your perspective and tap into your want power, ask yourself, "What would my best friend tell me to get me through this challenge?" It has been proven that your best friends will give you better advice than you can give yourself. With their outside perspective, they can see your challenge through a lens of objectivity and support. They will give you motivation to keep going, not beat yourself up

Being vulnerable is scary. You have a natural inclination to fear the worst, because that fear helped to keep our species safe millions of years ago. In today's world, though, being vulnerable usually isn't a case of life and death. And venturing outside of your comfort zone will lead you to incredible growth.

At what point, though, do your fears cease to be a figment of your imagination and start being real? Can you push too far outside of your comfort zone?

The Chaos Zone

Let's go back to the beginning of Brent's story. His comfort zone was when he was at home, not at the gym, and especially not lifting weights. So if he'd stayed at home, he would have been safe, secure, and free from any ridicule or embarrassment.

Instead, he chose to go to the gym by himself before he really knew what he was getting himself into. He wasn't comfortable with strength training, he wasn't comfortable going to the gym by himself, and he especially wasn't comfortable with those very difficult—and very dangerous—lifts that he did while at the gym. By doing all of these things that he was uncomfortable with, he was actually venturing too far out of his comfort zone into what author Geoff Colvin calls, "the chaos zone."

In his book *Talent is Overrated,* Colvin describes the chaos zone as the area so far outside of your comfort zone that you are almost doomed to fail if you go there. The chaos zone is where someone who has never spoken in public before does a speech in front of an audience of thousands, or someone who has never swung a golf club before decides to do eighteen holes at a professional golf course.

The result of this is almost assured failure, and can actually do more damage than staying in your comfort zone. Not only do you have to go through the agony of failure, but you also teach yourself that venturing outside of your comfort zone is just as scary as you thought it would be. Brent's experience at the gym would have resulted in him forever staying in his comfort zone had Arnold Schwarzenegger not chimed in and given him the proper perspective on the situation.

Too often when we set goals, we create a plan in comfort or chaos. You want to graduate from a university and get a good job, but you don't want the classes to be too hard. So you take the easiest classes, with the easiest professors, and enjoy your free time rather than taking on a part-time internship. Then you graduate and wonder why it is so difficult to find a job.

Or you go to the opposite end of the spectrum. You want to lose weight, so you try to lose ten pounds as soon as possible. You go from not exercising or watching what you eat to being on a strict diet and exercising every day. Then, after just a few days, you burn yourself out. You feel hopeless when you can't seem to summon the willpower to make it to the gym or resist the side of french fries.

Neither one of these paths will lead to success. To get on the right path to your goals, you need to find the middle ground: the learning zone.

The Learning Zone

Let's take one final look at Brent's story. In staying home, he was in the comfort zone, and in doing those complicated lifts, he was in the chaos zone. But what if Brent first focused on just becoming comfortable going to the gym by himself? Instead of doing two of the most difficult lifts there are, what if he instead focused on doing a lift he was already comfortable with? That would allow him to get over his fear of going to the gym by himself, still build some muscle, and become more confident in himself as a regular exerciser. That would push him just beyond his comfort zone without going too far, into the chaos zone. That would put him in the learning zone.

The learning zone is that place just beyond your current capabilities. It is where you are pushing yourself to learn and grow without setting yourself up for failure. To the person who wants to graduate from college, this means taking challenging courses and having an internship, without working forty hours per week and taking all honors classes. To the person who wants to lose ten pounds, this means starting by eating a healthy breakfast and exercising just one day per week, and making slow and consistent progress from there.

The learning zone is where your true growth occurs. It is where you venture outside of your comfort zone, do things you're not great at yet, and fail occasionally, but are able to learn from those mistakes instead of being defeated by them.

Getting to the Learning Zone

Getting to the learning zone requires both willpower and discipline. You need the willpower to push yourself beyond your comfort zone, both when you are planning for your goal and when you are in the process of achieving it. Venturing outside of your comfort zone can be scary. Even when you are just putting a plan to paper, you will naturally visualize what it will be like to go outside of your comfort zone, and it will likely make you nervous. You need your willpower to move past the nerves.

At the same time, however, you also need discipline to hold you back from wanting too much, too fast. As a member of the human race, you are naturally optimistic—even when it comes to leaving your comfort zone. This isn't because you don't fear vulnerability; it is because you have too much faith in your own willpower. Brent may have been afraid of going to the gym, but he was also far too optimistic about his ability to do the difficult lifts. Venturing outside of your comfort zone is a process, and you must have the discipline to take it step by step, rather than jumping headfirst into something you're not prepared for.

So what is the perfect place between the comfort zone and the chaos zone? How much should you be pushing yourself, and how much should you be holding back?

According to Daniel Coyle, author of *The Talent Code*, the "sweet spot" of the learning zone is when you are successful 60 to 80 percent of the time. As he says, "You don't want to be succeeding 40 percent of the time. That's flailing around. You don't want to be succeeding 95 percent of the time. That's too easy. You want to constantly be adjusting the environment so that you're succeeding 60 to 80 percent of the time."

Unfortunately, the learning zone isn't always pleasant. Only succeeding 60 to 80 percent of the time can be frustrating. But if you allow yourself to become fully engaged in the process of learning, then the learning zone can be very intrinsically motivating. You will enjoy improving in your domain much more than the ease you feel in the comfort zone. It will fill you with joy to see the "before" and "after" photos of your progress over time. You will gain confidence in yourself and find the motivation you need to take on the next challenge.

To help you get to this learning zone sweet spot, here are a number of strategies you can use:

1) *Focus on achieving small wins.* When Brent left for the gym, he was expecting a big win. A big win would have been getting there, doing all of those difficult lifts with perfect form, and making major progress toward his fitness goal. But as we know, in order to achieve that big win, he had to enter the chaos zone.

   That's why you want to focus on achieving small wins. Small wins are in the learning zone. They are realistic and attainable. If Brent had gone to the gym and done simpler lifts, that would have been in the learning zone and it would have been a small win.

2) *Chunking.* Another of our old strategies comes in handy in a big way in getting into the learning zone. The learning zone is—and should be—uncomfortable for you. It shouldn't be much fun. But that discomfort, boredom, and frustration will be worth it. And the best way to get through something that is difficult, but valuable, is to break it down into manageable chunks.

   If your goal is to learn a new language, just focus on studying for the next thirty minutes. If your goal is to lose weight, just focus on eating healthy for your next meal. If your goal is wake up earlier, just focus on making it out of bed and to the coffee pot. All of those may be difficult, but they're not impossible. You may fail sometimes, but you will mostly be successful.

3) *Be self-aware.* How do you hold back from entering the chaos zone? The best way is to simply be honest with yourself. Take a look at your prior attempts to achieve a goal. Did you try to bite off more than you could chew? If you're like most people, you probably were overly optimistic about your willpower in the past. Now is the time to make an honest assessment of yourself and use that information to create a plan. Look at your past behavior through an objective lens and see what would be a realistic step in the right direction.

4) *Have patience.* Along with being overly optimistic, you probably have a natural desire to get results as soon as possible. The reality of most situations, though, is that you probably don't need to get big results right away.

While taking a look at your past attempts to achieve your goals, ask yourself if you really needed to get flat abs in eight weeks. Or read a new book every week. Would you be in a better place today if instead you'd made small, consistent progress from when you started your last goal until now? If the answer is yes, then heed that lesson. Understand that real progress takes time. And if you commit to taking small steps outside of your comfort zone every single day, then you can simply allow time to take its course as your comfort zone slowly expands.

Personal growth has been a natural human motivation since we first needed to become better hunters and gatherers in order to survive. Deep down, we want to learn, we want to grow, and we want to improve our lives for the better. But growth isn't easy. You must be willing to push yourself outside of your comfort zone while also holding yourself back from trying to do too much.

Pushing Beyond Your Limits

Robic was about two-thirds of the way through the race in 2004 when he finally believed he just could not keep pushing. Despite his ability to ignore his brain's messages, despite his crew's motivation, and despite his unbelievable endurance, he was just flat-out exhausted.

Then his best friend and crew member Miran Stanovnik brought up Robic's childhood. He had a tough upbringing. His father beat him and said that he would never amount to anything. Later, Robic joined the Slovenian military, where he was treated poorly by the officers and made to feel like he was lower than dirt.

These past hardships were what created the spark inside of Robic that made him want to get into cycling in the first place. He wanted to show everyone who didn't believe in him that he could amount to something. He wanted to prove he was a champion. So, with tears streaming down his face, Stanovnik shouted at Robic, "You show Slovenia, you show the army, you show the world what you are!"

Robic got a sudden burst of energy. While his best friend continued to yell words of pride and love, he pushed on like a madman for over two hours. His best friend's reminder of *why* he was doing this in the first place was enough to keep him pushing. It was enough to keep him enduring a level of pain and fatigue we can only imagine. And he did it while still maintaining the proper speed.

Whatever your inspiring purpose is, do not underestimate it. Fall deeply in love with it. It has the power to help you on your path, even when other people may call you foolish. It has the power to keep you working on your goal day after day, even when it appears that you have reached rock bottom. And it has the power to give you the strength to push your limits and keep fighting.

When you reach the limits of what you feel like you are capable of, remember your vision. Hold onto the image of what you know in your heart is possible. Then use that rush of want power to push you beyond what you thought were your limits—then see what you are actually capable of accomplishing.

Conclusion

Robic proved that your mind can hold you back if you let it. But by leaving decisions like speed, food, and breaks up to his support crew, he demonstrated how to train yourself to ignore your brain's messages of pain and fatigue. By remembering what he was fighting for, he could keep pushing himself even further—and you can, too.

When you feel like you have reached your limits, remember your higher purpose. Remember *why* you are fighting, and remember that the pain you are feeling is worth it. This will inspire you to keep going even when things seem to be at their absolute worst. It will push you out of your comfort zone and into the learning zone, where your goals become reality.

Key Points

- *Fatigue is not biological—it is emotional.* Like fear or anxiety, fatigue is in the mind. It motivates you to stop exercising the same way anxiety motivates you to stay away from public speaking. And just like you can will yourself to overcome fear, you can will yourself to push far beyond your first feelings of exhaustion.

- *You have more willpower than you think.* You may feel exhausted and helpless to avoid giving in to short-term desires, but you can still will yourself to do the right thing.

- *Progress can be broken down into the comfort zone, the chaos zone, and the learning zone.* The comfort zone is where tasks are so easy and safe that you don't progress at all. The chaos zone is where everything is so hard and frightening that you can't learn from your mistakes. The learning zone is where everything is challenging and uncomfortable, yet it's also achievable. You fail 20 to 40 percent of the time, but you're able to learn from that failure and grow. The learning zone is the place where you want to be.

Strategies

1) *Make an honest assessment of your progress.* When were things too easy? When were things too hard? When were you able to make consistent progress?

2) *Find your learning zone "sweet spot."* Find that place where you were challenged but not overwhelmed. It should be uncomfortable, but achievable.

3) *Remove the decision to quit.* When you find the sweet spot, remove the option to quit. Robic pushed his comfort zone because he had no choice. By removing the option to quit—and fully committing to your goal—your brain will focus your willpower on persevering, rather than finding excuses..

Part IV

The Journey to Greatness

Chapter 9

The Long Term

"It takes twenty years to build a reputation and five minutes to ruin it. If you think about that, you'll act differently."
– Warren Buffett

"This is it!" thought a young Warren Buffett as he picked up *The Intelligent Investor*—the book that would change his life. Before he read the book, he wasn't what many would consider a success. He was a rebellious kid who hated "pointless" schoolwork and hated his living situation. His family had moved from Omaha to Washington, DC, when his father was elected to Congress, and Buffett fell in with a bad group of kids there.

He skipped his schoolwork, leading to poor grades. He grew angry with his parents and ran away from home. He even shoplifted sporting goods that he sold on the black market. But underneath all of those petty acts of rebellion was one glimmer of hope: Buffett knew he was going to be a successful businessman.

At the age of eleven, he bought his first stock, later regretting that he didn't get into the market earlier. At the age of thirteen, he bought a paper route and made enough money that he actually had to file his own tax return—making sure to write off his bicycle as a business expense. He continued to explore new ventures like selling racing tip sheets and pinball machines. Then, at the age of fifteen, he became a property owner, buying a forty-acre Nebraska farm. Over the next four years, he continued to make various investments in real estate, coin-operated machines, and the stock market.

But that all came grinding to a halt when he picked up *The Intelligent Investor.* This book—and the more thorough version titled *Security Analysis*—explained in depth the "holes" in the stock market. It showed how an intelligent investor could find companies that the market undervalued. It explained that the market placed too much emphasis on metrics such as earnings per share, and how somebody could find stocks that seemed to be dead but that really had one last breath of life for their investors.

When Buffett read that book, he realized how much opportunity he had been missing out on. Just as he regretted not making an investment before age eleven, he also regretted having wasted all of his time and money on stocks that were overvalued. He vowed at that moment that he would not make another investment until he understood every line of the 725-page book.

So he read the book again, and again...and again. He willed himself to read the book *twelve times* before making another investment. That decision was one of the best of his life, as it did not just change his investing success; it changed his life success.

After turning that book into his personal investing bible, Buffett sought to learn as much as he could from its author, Benjamin Graham. After graduating from the University of Nebraska, Buffett applied to get his MBA from Columbia University in New York. Graham was a professor at Columbia, and Buffett was determined to become his student. And in 1951, Buffett enrolled in Graham's class, giving him the opportunity to learn from the brilliant man firsthand.

Buffett seized his moment to impress his hero. He answered every question Graham asked the class, even reciting lines from Graham's own book. Graham could not help but be impressed by Buffett's knowledge and commitment to Graham's own philosophy of investing, making him consider mentoring the young man.

Until that point, Graham had been committed primarily to mentoring young Jewish students; when he was a young Jewish man himself trying to make it on Wall Street, Graham faced extreme prejudice from the investment community because of his heritage. But that priority changed when he met Buffett. Here was a kid who knew his philosophy as well as he did, and probably could recite his book even better. So Graham decided to take Buffett under his wing.

From that point on, Buffett would learn from, work for, and even challenge many of Graham's ideas to form his own investment philosophy—a philosophy that would turn him into the richest man in the world. Buffett's philosophy does not require understanding of complicated algorithms, derivatives, or technology. All it requires is willpower.

Buffett's Boring Approach

Buffett claims that he has been "hardwired since birth to allocate capital." However, while his passion for investing is certainly real, his story proves that he cannot claim that talent alone is what led to his success. In reality, it was his willpower. Once Buffett realized the value of *The Intelligent Investor* and *Security Analysis*, he used his willpower to read them over and over again until he knew every aspect of the books. He understood them so well that he could quote from the texts even better than the man who wrote them.

Now you may think that, given his passion for investing, he probably enjoyed the book. Reading it must have been pleasurable for him, not boring. And that may have been true for the first, second, or even the sixth read. But reading the exact same textbook material on the eleventh or twelfth pass must have bored even Buffett. But he chose to *embrace* that boredom because he understood how important the information he was reading was.

This idea of embracing boredom set the tone for Buffett's entire investing career. He was willing to read about boring industries like textiles and manufacturing, while others were seduced by more exciting companies like those in technology. He was willing to do extensive research on the actual companies he was buying, rather than simply placing a bet on an unknown stock. And he was willing to choose companies based on their long-term prospects rather than their immediate potential payoffs.

As Yahoo Finance wrote, "If Buffett's 'formula' could be described in a word, that word would be 'boring.' Wonderfully, profitably, enjoyably boring."

You have learned by now that hard work alone is not always what separates the truly excellent performers from the rest. Those like Buffett who achieve greatness do not just work hard; they work hard on the dry, boring things that no one else wants to do. And they have the patience to stick with them for the long term.

The Will to Be Patient

Buffett's success can be attributed to his won't power as much as it can his will power. While the bull markets and the potential "quick scores" excited others, he held back his capital during boom times, always fearful that a crash was right around the corner. As a result, he didn't bet big on the technology booms of the twentieth century. He didn't bet big on the Internet. And he held on to large amounts of cash, waiting until the market crashed and he could buy companies for cheap.

Despite the apparent growth that was on the table, he was never impulsive. Everything he did was calculated to maximize his opportunity and minimize his chances of losing vast amounts of capital. The best example of this was when he read *The Intelligent Investor* and vowed that he would not invest again until he knew every aspect of both it and *Security Analysis*. After reading those books, he saw he was missing opportunities, and he had the will to hold back until he learned how to make the most of his capital.

It is tempting to want big results fast. Whether those results are in the stock market, in our waistlines, or in any other goal, we want things to happen now! That is why so many of us overdo it. We try to quit smoking, lose weight, and get ahead in our careers, all at the same time. But you must hold back your desire to change everything at once and embrace the long run. Small changes over long periods of time equal big improvements. That is why a young Buffett devised what he called "the Snowball."

The Snowball

Where would you be today if you'd saved just one dollar at a 2 percent interest rate every day since you graduated from high school? If that was ten years ago, you'd be $5,807 richer. If that was twenty years ago, you'd be $12,887 richer. If that was thirty years ago, you'd be $21,517 richer. And that's just one dollar per day. Those numbers would more than double if you had saved two dollars per day.

Okay, I'm probably not shocking you with these figures. If you have taken high-school math, you know the long-term value of compound interest.

But let's start applying this concept to goals other than saving money. Where would you be today if you'd spent twenty minutes per day for the last year exercising? Where would you be today if you'd spent those twenty minutes learning a new language? Where would you be today if you'd just eaten a healthy breakfast every morning?

Every year, millions of us forget about the idea of small changes accumulating into big results and instead set huge goals on New Year's Eve. We set goals to quit smoking, eat healthy, exercise, and spend more time with our family—all at once. Then, after just a few weeks, our willpower muscles are exhausted and we are completely burned out. We are left feeling helpless, like we'll never achieve our goals and dreams—that is, of course, until next New Year's, when we begin the cycle again.

What if, instead, every year you were to simply make one small, realistic change to your daily routine that over time would lead to extraordinary results?

This could be exercising twenty minutes per day, writing twenty minutes per day, or carving out twenty minutes per day to make your family a priority. Every year, you could then add one more thing to your list. How would your life be different today if you'd spent the last five years doing that? This is what Buffett called his "snowball"—and it is a fail-proof system for achieving great results.

As you know, a snowball grows every time it rolls over. But while it may add the same 12 percent more snow with each rotation, that 12 percent is a bigger total amount of snow each time. At an early age, Buffett learned that the exact same phenomenon could happen for his wealth.

So he set his sights on 12 percent growth per year and did everything within his power to hit that number. This meant pushing himself to see opportunities during hard economic times and holding back from potential opportunities in the marketplace during boom times. Having such discipline took willpower and led to phenomenal results over the course of his life.

Great results take time, patience, and the willpower to focus on consistency rather than intensity. Unfortunately, most of us go against this idea of slow progress. In school, kids slack off for most of the semester, then try to cram everything in at the last minute. In their free time, people try a new skill, like playing the piano, but give up quickly if they feel they have no "natural gift" for it. And in their work, employees try to multitask, which leads to many in-process projects and nothing getting completed.

This short attention span not only works against your brain's natural abilities, but it actually begins to swing power back to your primitive brain. When you multitask or don't persist with anything, you become more easily distracted. You focus more on short-term pleasures and weaken your ability to stick with your long-term goals. By consistently multitasking or trying to take shortcuts, you set yourself up for failure both now and in the future.

Why is it so tempting to go against the values of the long term? Why do we ignore the benefits of slow progress and seek big results, ASAP? The answer lies in a phenomenon called "the planning fallacy."

The Planning Fallacy

The test was simple. The participants, all non-exercisers with the goal of adding workouts to their weekly routines, were asked to write down how many hours they planned to spend in the gym over the next two weeks. After each participant recorded the amount of time they *planned* to spend in the gym, they would then record how much time they *actually* spent in the gym. After careful calculation, the participants on average planned to spend about twenty hours working out over the two weeks.

You may have gone through a similar planning process at some point, so you probably won't be shocked when I tell you that the average time these people actually spent in the gym wasn't even half their prediction. The participants only spent an average of about eight hours exercising during the two-week period.

But that's not the study's most shocking finding. After the two weeks were up, the researchers were curious to see if people would learn from their behavior, so they asked the participants to start fresh and plan how much time they would spend in the gym over the next two weeks. Surely, they thought, people would realize what was realistic this time around and plan accordingly.

Nope. Rather than learning from their past behavior, the participants planned to spend *even more* time in the gym. In their minds, the previous two weeks were an anomaly and their "true selves" were going to show up and make it to the gym for twenty-five hours this time.

This experiment reveals what researchers call "the planning fallacy." As humans, we are incredibly optimistic by nature, so when we set plans, we overestimate our abilities. Psychologist Roger Buehler discovered this in 1994 when he did an experiment with his graduate students.

Thirty-seven students were asked to estimate how long it would take them to finish their senior theses. They were to make three time predictions based on different scenarios: First, if everything went as well as it possibly could, which the students predicted would take them 27.4 days; second, if everything went as poorly as it possibly could, which they predicted would take 48.6 days; and finally, what they thought would actually happen, which they believed would take 33.9 days. Then they were to measure their predictions against how long it actually took them. The average actual completion time was 55.5 days—a whole week longer than the prediction for if everything went as poorly as it possibly could.

Buehler theorized that the reason we overestimate our abilities is that we are all wishful thinkers. We want to believe that things will work out for the best, so even our worst-case scenarios aren't that bad. That is why, despite a 40 percent divorce rate, newlyweds believe they have no chance of divorce; and despite a 30 percent chance of getting cancer, the average person only believes he has a 10 percent chance. We still believe that goal failure, divorce, or disease can happen—we just don't believe it will happen to us.

Although there are many proven advantages to being optimistic, the planning fallacy is dangerous. What do you think the chances are that those exercisers were able to establish their exercise routine after four consecutive weeks of not hitting their planned goals? Slim to none. They probably felt more like failures with every planned workout missed, leading them to give up hope.

The worst part of this thinking is that, usually, we don't need our most optimistic estimates to be true in order to be successful.

The study participants did not need twenty-plus hours of exercise. Had they planned on even doing five hours of exercise over the two-week period, it would have been a big improvement over nothing. By being overly optimistic, they entered the chaos zone and set themselves up for assured failure.

Luckily, there is a strategy you can use to beat the planning fallacy and get back on the "Buffett-track" to long-term success: reference class forecasting. Reference class forecasting is taking the results of the past and using them to predict the future. If the non-exercisers had used the results from their first two weeks of exercise to develop a more realistic approach to their next two weeks, they would have used this method.

The key with reference class forecasting is to avoid the trap of thinking that the future is going to be "special." The non-exercisers believed that the second two weeks would be somehow different than the first two, leading to their second round of unrealistic plans. When you plan for the future, you need to understand that it will be much more like the past than like your optimistic projections. Your past results are the best predictor of your future. And if you end up doing better than you have in the past, it will only serve to give you more confidence as you move toward your goals.

That only leaves you the challenge of bridging the gap between your plans and getting started. And to do that, you need to beat procrastination.

Why We Procrastinate

There you sit. You have the goal in front of you, but you are not quite sure how to proceed. You have visualized what this project will look like when it is finished, and you cannot wait to see it completed. But for whatever reason, it just does not feel like the right time to get started. You feel a little "off." You do not know exactly where to start, and there is not enough time on your schedule to get everything done. You think to yourself, *You know what? Tomorrow would be a much better time to do this.*

No matter what project you are working on, we all follow this script. A whopping 95 percent of people admit to procrastinating at least some of the time—and the other 5 percent are lying. To procrastinate is human, but it is also dangerous.

Procrastination does not just prevent things from getting done, but it also adds an extraordinary level of stress to your life. In a study of college students, those who procrastinated the most—even the ones who claimed to "work best under pressure"—performed worse on every single academic measure. They were also much more likely to get sick from the stress, all-nighters, and junk food they ate while cramming for their final exams.

Where does this desire to procrastinate come from? Researchers have found three sources that, depending on your personality, increase your likelihood to procrastinate:

- *Impulsiveness.* You may be excited when you visualize your project, but when the monotony of the process comes, you get bored with it. To escape the boredom and improve your mood, you choose to do something more fun: You put off the term paper until tomorrow to play a video game right now. You put off your jog to spend time at a happy hour with colleagues after work. And you put off cleaning the garage to watch the next episode of your favorite TV show.

  Procrastination due to impulsiveness is the most dangerous form. In fact, the people who report the highest level of chronic procrastination are those who are the most impulsive.

- *Delay discounting.* Because your brain is wired for survival, you value rewards that are right in front of you much more than ones that are abstract or that you have to wait for. After all, your brain doesn't know if you'll live to see tomorrow. So "the bird in the hand" is much more valuable than the "two in the bush." This is why countless experiments show that people will take $50 today rather than $100 a month from now.

This is a phenomenon called "delay discounting," and it is another key reason why you might be tempted to procrastinate. You may not even find much pleasure in watching TV or browsing the Internet, but if you can do them right now and procrastinate work that will only pay off in the future, they seem much more fun. This also means that if you try to be productive now and use a future reward to incent you, it will seem less appealing (Frisbee doesn't seem as fun when you have to wait four hours to play).

- *Perfectionism.* We have an amazing ability to visualize the future. This has given us the inspiration to build pyramids, cathedrals, and skyscrapers. But when you focus your attention on these huge works of beauty, you can feel discouraged and lose motivation when you start laying the foundation and see how far you are from achieving your goal.

  This leaves you feeling impatient, anxious, and hopeless. To avoid these feelings, you are tempted to put the work off for another time. You hope that if you put the work off until tomorrow, you will get over these feelings and be able to make some real progress. Or, even worse, you might put the work off forever because you feel like any effort you put toward your goal is hopeless. You may start believing that you will never be able to create the beautiful, perfect project that you have in your mind.

These tendencies to procrastinate leave us in an obvious bind, as it is difficult to properly motivate ourselves to buckle down and get to work. So what strategies can you use to defeat procrastination?

Defeating Procrastination

Imagine that the clock has just struck five o'clock on Wednesday afternoon, and you take a look at your gym bag. You are filled with utter disgust. The last thing you want to do tonight is work out. You have been trying to create a regular exercise habit for years now, but no matter how hard you try, nothing works.

On Sunday night, when you're planning your schedule for the week ahead, you are always positive. You plan to go to the gym after work three days per week and get excited at the prospect of a newer, slimmer body. However, by the time the bell tolls and you actually have to go to the gym, that motivation is nowhere to be found. Instead, you are stressed, tired, and craving a night of take-out food and TV to help you get over the day.

You have now shifted your brain to envisioning two different scenarios that may take place this evening: sucking it up and going to the gym, or skipping the gym and having a night of relaxation.

First, you consider staying strong and going to the gym. You initially feel good about yourself for making that decision, but then you envision the miles on the treadmill that you will have to do. You remember the pain of your previous run and the boredom of watching the clock go by so slowly.

Then something odd begins to happen. Your brain actually sends messages down to your muscles that make them begin to feel even more sore and fatigued than before. The brain remembers pain more than it remembers pleasure, so it is easier for it to remember the stress of the last run—and the amount of willpower you exerted—rather than the sense of pride you felt when you finished. Now, even though you haven't moved from your desk, simply envisioning this scenario is making you feel more tired. With every minute you picture that scenario, both the pain messages and your temptation to procrastinate increase.

Then you begin to envision your night on the couch with the take-out food in hand. You think about how good the food will taste and how nice it will be to catch up on your favorite TV show. You begin to anticipate having the night off to relax and ease your stress. It seems like paradise.

Then another odd thing happens. When you start to anticipate the delicious food and relaxation, your brain releases our old friend dopamine. For all your brain knows, getting that take-out food could be a matter of life and death! So, the dopamine activates your reward center and makes you begin to *crave* the night at home on the couch, which your brain now wants you to have at all costs.

On top of everything else, the simple act of envisioning these two scenarios is also causing your brain to burn through its supply of glucose. The longer you contemplate the decision, the more glucose you use up, leaving you with less willpower fuel to push yourself to go to the gym and lowering your chances of making it there.

So simply thinking about these two scenarios is causing your brain to (1) make your muscles feel more fatigued than they really are, (2) crave the food you want to order, (3) make you want to ease your stress through relaxation, and (4) deplete the total amount of glucose that you have to exert willpower. With all of this happening, is it any wonder that you and many others will probably procrastinate? Especially when you think you can always make up for it later?

This story is one that we have all experienced at some point. It may not have been a trip to the gym you tried to skip, but perhaps a night of studying or a night of working on chores. Whatever your goal, the minute that you started envisioning what you had planned to do versus your much less stressful alternative, you began to set yourself up for failure.

Anytime you contemplate whether to stick to your goals or take a break from them, you lower your willpower. That simple act of contemplation makes it much more likely that you will procrastinate, take a break, and fail to establish great habits. As you can see, once you begin to envision exerting your willpower in the future, you begin to set yourself up for failure.

There is a simple way to avoid this fate: keeping your mind in the present. There is very little suffering in the present. Think back to the last time you were on a treadmill; was it the running that was painful? Or was it watching the clock and wishing you were done? Do you suffer at work when you are fully immersed in what you are doing? Or only when you are watching the clock in anticipation of going home?

Whatever you exert your willpower for, you put yourself through unnecessary pain by envisioning it in the future. Even if you were able to stay strong and make it to the gym, for example, you would arrive with fatigued muscles, a short-term mindset, and lower willpower to push yourself through your workout.

Staying in the present, of course, is easier said than done. It is not easy to prevent your mind from wandering to the future and beginning to anticipate pain or a short-term reward. That is where meditation comes in. As you know, meditation is the fastest, simplest, and most effective way to train your mind to focus on the present and lower your chances of procrastinating. So the next time you're in a similar situation to the example above, take a deep breath. Bring yourself to the present, and focus on accomplishing your goal one step at a time.

Being Mindful of the Present, Past, and Future

When the Internet boom of the late 1990s was in full force, Warren Buffett stood up in front of hundreds of investors, analysts, and tech-company CEOs to weigh in on why he was *not* going to invest in Internet companies.

"Investors these days are expecting far too much out of their companies, and I'm going to explain why," he began.

The crowd, which was full of men and women who had doubled, tripled, or even sextupled their portfolios over the prior few years were shocked by the statement. Then Buffett went on to explain how the market had reacted to technology booms of the past and why investors didn't usually come out ahead.

To make his point, he brought up the invention of the automobile. Like the Internet, cars were a complete game-changer. The car industry completely disrupted transportation of not only people, but also goods and services. It allowed people to begin to move out of cities, which led to suburbanization. Suburbanization led to a boom in the housing market, and so on. In response to this boom, over 2,000 car companies were started in America alone. And if you were to look at how popular cars are even today, you would probably say, "Get in on cars!"

At the time of Buffett's speech, however, there were only three remaining American car companies—none of which were very good stocks to own. Despite the industry's impact, despite its importance, and despite the seemingly huge riches that would come from cars, investing in cars did not pay off for investors.

Buffett used this information to inform his prediction about the Internet. And sure enough, just two years after his speech, the bubble burst. Thousands of Internet companies went bankrupt. And for every Amazon.com that made investors millions, there were hundreds of other e-commerce sites that lost all of their investors' money. Then, when the market corrected itself and stocks were dirt cheap, the patient Buffett seized the moment to start getting in on the Internet boom.

In this chapter, we have discussed the advantages and disadvantages of having your thoughts in the present, the past, and the future. Warren Buffett's long-term strategy did not come from being able to predict the future through some genius. It came from looking at what happened in the past, using that information to predict the future, and having the discipline to not get caught up in the hype and expect huge results in the present. Even though

Buffett was always rolling his snowball toward a remarkable future, he learned from the past and used the information to make intelligent decisions in the present.

When you are working toward a goal, you will be tempted to act like the investors who were seeking the immediate big payoff. You will want the fast and easy results in your health, your career, and your finances. But you must remember that those quick results are an illusion. Even if you make fast initial progress, chances are good that your own bubble will burst and you will not be able to make it sustainable.

Instead, take on the Buffett mindset. Look to your past to see that anytime you try to get big results fast, it just ends with failure. Notice instead that if you simply start small and begin building your snowball, you will be far better off. Have patience. Buffett didn't become the richest man in the world overnight.

Conclusion

Warren Buffett is often cited as being a child prodigy who was wired from birth with extraordinary investing talent. After all, what eleven-year-old invests in the stock market? What fifteen-year-old owns property?

But saying that it was talent alone that led to Buffett's success dismisses entirely the willpower that he used to become the investing powerhouse we know today. He may have been talented, but he also had the willpower to do the boring things others wouldn't, to hold back from being impulsive, and to look to the past to set his goals for the future—and you can do the same.

Key Points

- *The key to long-term success is to build your "snowball."* Instead of getting caught in boom-and-bust cycles, Buffett's goal was to grow his wealth like a snowball—small at first, but making progress every year. This same analogy can be used for your goals. Instead of trying to improve everything at once, strive for consistent progress, always adding to your previous results.

- *Watch out for the planning fallacy.* You are naturally overly optimistic about how much you can accomplish. When you create a plan, you will be tempted to set yourself up for failure. To avoid this, you must look at your past results as the best predictor of your future abilities.

- *Whatever your reason, everyone procrastinates.* You might procrastinate because you are impulsive, a perfectionist, or don't value the large long-term reward as much as the small reward right in front of you. Regardless of the reason, everyone procrastinates.

- *You can defeat procrastination by keeping your mind in the present.* Whatever work you're tempted to procrastinate, you will drain your willpower by thinking about it ahead of time. Don't build up the boredom, exhaustion, or frustration you think will come with that work. Keep your mind in the present and take it step by step.

Strategies

1) *Think of a snowball that will help you reach your goal.* What activity can you do consistently to help you grow your snowball and achieve your purpose? Think long term.

2) *Combine the snowball with your daily win.* The long term is intimidating. To help your mind stay in the present, try to break down your snowball into daily wins.

3) *Do a reference-class forecast.* Before you overload your days, take an honest look back at your past successes and failures. What were you actually able to accomplish on a daily basis?

Chapter 10

The Pursuit of Perfection

"Perfection is not attainable. But if we chase perfection, we can catch excellence."
– Vince Lombardi

In 1959, Vince Lombardi finally got the chance he had worked all his life for: He was now the head coach of a National Football League (NFL) team. Unfortunately, that team was the Green Bay Packers. In those days, Green Bay was the NFL equivalent of Siberia. It was a horrible team, in an unknown city that happened to be almost as cold as Siberia. But Lombardi was nothing but grateful for the position. It was his opportunity to prove himself to the world.

Lombardi grew up in New York as the son of a poor Italian immigrant and faced discrimination for most of his life. Back then, Italian-Americans were thought of as hard workers but "dumb as dirt"—far too dumb for Lombari's dream job as a professional head football coach.

So the young Lombardi wasn't able to get a job at the professional level, or the college level, or even with a top high school team. The only place he could get a job as a coach was St. Cecilia High School, a small Catholic school with equally small players.

He had his work cut out for him. Somehow, he would have to prove that he could win championships with this group of average players if he ever wanted to reach his dream. So he fully committed himself to the task. He spent countless hours learning the strategy of the game and how to become a great leader. This hard work helped Lombardi lead his team to the state championship every year he was the head coach, including winning an unprecedented thirty-two games in a row.

He won so much in football that he was also asked to coach the basketball team, despite having never played the sport. And as with football, he created champions. Again, he led the team to the state championship in his first year as coach—because for him, it was not about a brilliant strategy, it was about bringing the best out of his players.

These remarkable results gave Lombardi the confidence to go to the next level of coaching. But despite his success, he was not considered by many university programs for roles as even an assistant coach. Only his alma mater, Fordham University, would give him a chance.

Fordham gave him the offensive coaching position, and as he had done for the past decade, Lombardi created winners. He coached his offense to be one of the best in the country. Surely, he thought, such results at the college level would prove his value and show that he could take on a head coaching responsibility. But both Fordham and other schools at which he interviewed made it clear that would never happen. Lombardi was continually turned down for head coaching jobs he was qualified for. One interviewer even told him, "You'd better look around and find something else, because I'm convinced no one is going to hire an Italian head coach."

So Lombardi was forced to turn to another school where it seemed as if every assistant coach was bred to become a head coach one day: West Point Military Academy, also known as "Army." Red Blaik, the head coach at Army, offered Lombardi a job running his offense. After being given the position, Lombardi proved his worth. He worked tirelessly to once again create the best offense in all of college football—and he did.

In Lombardi's first two seasons with Army, they only lost one game. They were among the best offenses in the country, and

Lombardi was sure that these results at the college level would finally be enough to earn him his dream job. But he was still denied. For the next five years, Lombardi languished as he saw his less-qualified peers continue to get the jobs he felt he deserved—until, finally, a glimmer of hope appeared.

The NFL's New York Giants were in search of a new head coach, and they sought Blaik to fill the position. Blaik turned it down, but recommended the team offer the position to Lombardi. The Giants were impressed by Lombardi but were still not willing to offer him anything more than a job running their offense. It was not Lombardi's ideal position, but at least he would be coaching at the highest level. So he took the job.

In the NFL, Lombardi learned the difference between coaching college players and coaching professionals. Professionals did not take as well to Lombardi's disciplinarian approach to the game. But like he had done all of his career, he found the right way to bring out the best in his players. Beyond creating a great offensive strategy, he created a drive in his players to become the best they could be.

In his second year with the Giants, he helped them get to the NFL Championship Game. The game was one of the first national broadcasts ever for the NFL, which meant that for the first time, Lombardi's brilliant coaching skills were on display for the entire nation. After the notoriety from that game, Lombardi was invited to interview with the lowly Green Bay Packers. He felt he could no longer linger as an assistant. It was time to become a head coach—no matter how terrible the team. And he achieved a bittersweet victory as he was finally offered a position as the head coach of the Green Bay Packers.

Seizing the Moment

Lombardi inherited a terrible situation in Green Bay. The team had finished the previous season in dead last. They had ten consecutive losing seasons and showed no signs of improvement. It was so bad that the once-proud franchise was actually considering moving away from its small northern home.

Things were bleak, but Lombardi was not intimidated. He came to the team with a passion and drive that shocked the players. He'd worked incredibly hard to get to that point, and if he failed, he knew he would never get another chance. It was do or die—for the Packers, and for him. So he walked into his first team meeting on a mission, saying, "Gentlemen, we are going to relentlessly chase perfection, knowing full well we will not catch it, because nothing is perfect. But we are going to relentlessly chase it. Because in the process, we will catch excellence. I'm not even remotely interested in being just good."

This speech captivated the team, especially the starting quarterback, Bart Starr, who later said, "I couldn't even sit in my chair I was so excited!"

Then they got to work. They worked harder, longer, and with more intensity than any other team in professional football. "I've done two boot camps in the Marines, and those didn't even come close to how hard Lombardi's practices were. We couldn't believe it, we just thought this guy was crazy," said Gary Knafelc, one of the star Green Bay players.

"Guys would lose consciousness right there on the field. There was vomiting, and it wouldn't be uncommon to see a guy just keel over," said Jerry Kramer, another player on the team. "He wanted every ounce of ability you had, and he would not relent until you gave it to him."

Typically, this type of coaching is done at the high school or college level when players need to learn discipline and improve their fitness. It was unheard of to put professionals through that kind of torture during practices. Yet these professionals loved playing for Lombardi. He knew how to motivate his players to become the absolute best they could be.

"I remember sitting there, hand in my chin, thinking, 'I'm never going to play for this guy.' Then he came up to me and said, 'Son, one of these days you're going to be the best guard in all of football.' That started my motor. With that comment, he allowed me to think about being a great football player," remembered Kramer.

The relentless work, discipline, and motivation paid off. It was do or die—and Lombardi did. In their first season, Lombardi turned a hopeless team into a winner, finishing the year with seven wins and five losses. After that, the Green Bay Packers became a perennial powerhouse. The next year, they made it all the way to the NFL Championship Game, falling just nine yards short of a touchdown that would have secured them the victory.

But that loss would prove irrelevant, as they won five championships over the next seven years—something no other team in NFL history has done. In the process, the city of Green Bay became nicknamed "Title Town," and Vince Lombardi became legendary. And the name of the man once thought too stupid to be a head coach is now on the trophy given to the winner of the Super Bowl every year: "The Lombardi Trophy."

Never Settle

Vince Lombardi is remembered as one of the greatest coaches in the history of football. Given all his success, it is amazing to think that he was so close to never even becoming a coach at the college level. But before Lombardi, there were no Italian head coaches on any level. So let's break down Lombardi's story to see what he did differently to become the first.

After the Packers lost to the Philadelphia Eagles in Lombardi's first-ever championship game as a head coach, he addressed his team: "Gentlemen, we got beat today. But I can tell you right now, we will never lose a championship game again."

And they never did. This response represents how Lombardi responded every time he was denied what he truly wanted in life. In all of those instances when he was passed over for head coaching positions, or was told that no one was going to hire an Italian head coach, he never accepted that fate.

It would have been easy for him to say, "Well, if I have the results, if I have the experience, and they still won't hire me, then I guess it just isn't meant to be. At least I still get to be an assistant coach"—giving up on his dream and settling into an easy, comfortable life.

But Lombardi knew he was meant for something more. He knew he could lead a team to greater heights as a head coach. It was his destiny. So he never celebrated good results when he knew great results were possible. He held onto the pain of not reaching his true potential and used it as motivation to push even harder.

Your primitive brain is hardwired to take the easy path. It wants to settle. It wants to be comfortable and safe. And oftentimes, the motivation to take the safe and comfortable path is even justified by the modern brain through practicality. The practical answer for Lombardi was to give up on his dream of becoming a head coach and settle for a job as an assistant. On your journey, you will be tempted to do the same.

What ultimately stops you from achieving your dream may not be failure. It is far more likely that it will be settling. You will get 75 percent of the way there and see a comfortable way out. You will be given opportunities to settle for the good things you already have, rather than work for the great things you know are possible. Do not be seduced by this path. There is no shame in living a comfortable life if that is what you truly want. But be honest with yourself; if you dream of more, do not lose sight of it. Don't settle for what's practical; work for what's possible.

Principles

Vince Lombardi did not stick to the status quo. His first speech as a head coach was to a team that finished dead last in the league, yet the speech was about chasing perfection. What right did a first-time head coach talking to a team of losers have to chase perfection?

But the pursuit of perfection was one of Lombardi's principles. He didn't care about the team's record last season, he didn't care about its inexperience, and he didn't care about what others thought he should say as head coach. He cared about helping his players become the best they could possibly be. That is why he put them through painfully tough practices. That is why he made them show up fifteen minutes early for everything. And that is why he kept pushing them even after they became a winning team. He never made decisions based on what others were doing; he made decisions based on deep principles that he had developed over a lifetime. And his strong principles were a big part of his strong willpower.

Unfortunately, "principles" are thrown around far too often without people truly understanding their meaning. One of the best definitions of a principle comes from Stephen Covey, author of *The 7 Habits of Highly Effective People*: "A principle is a natural law like gravity...principles are objective....If you drop something, gravity controls. If I don't tell you the truth, you won't trust me—that's a natural law."

In other words, principles are objective laws that are a part of your unique character. Some examples are always keeping your word, always being kind and respectful, and always working hard. Ideally, your principles represent your purpose, your priorities, and the person you want to live up to every day. There is intrinsic motivation to stick to these principles because at our core, we all want to be the best versions of ourselves.

How Principles Affect Willpower

"Does it really matter if I skip it today? It's just one day." At some point in your life, you have said those words. You were exhausted, stressed, or focused on something else, and you didn't want to work toward your goals that day. This happens to me all the time. It's always near the end of the day, when my routine has been thrown off and the last thing I want to do is go to the gym, read, meditate, or whatever I'm supposed to be doing. I just want to relax on the couch, watch some TV, and go to bed. But when I feel this way, I remember always three of my principles:

- Do the little things right.

- Do not endorse any practice that I am not willing to do myself.

- I always have the willpower to do what is right.

Then, all of a sudden, I get a rush of energy and it isn't nearly as hard to summon the willpower that I need to get things done. I am able to harness my want power and work on what I know I should be doing. This is because my principles are the guidelines that I have set to achieve my purpose in life. They represent what I truly want, and therefore it requires less willpower for me to stick to them.

Having a set of principles will make it easier for you to work toward your purpose and identify with the best version of yourself. As you continue to identify more with this version through your principles, you will begin to become your best self.

The caveat, of course, is that you must truly believe in each principle. If you put something on your list that you are not passionate about, you will not be able to find the want power that you need to stick to it.

How to Determine Your Principles

Unfortunately, there is no scientifically proven ideal method to determine what your principles are. Each person is different, and we all value different things. We all have different moral, spiritual, and familial priorities. But here is a step-by-step method that you can follow to get you started thinking about what your true principles are:

1) *Schedule quiet time.* You will need to completely unplug yourself from the outside world. You do not want any distracting thoughts or communications that may intrude on this time of serious self-reflection. So take care of everything you need to do. Get to a place where the outside world won't need to contact you for at least several hours.

2) *Take the objective approach.* One of the biggest problems people face when coming up with principles is thinking too much about what they "should" write down. They think about what their family, friends, or culture believes they should value and write that down. While these may be good things, if you do not truly believe in what you're writing, you will not stick to it when it is inevitably challenged. So take an objective approach in how you view yourself. To do this, try to study yourself as if you were an entirely new species, separate from all human and societal norms. Then ask questions: What is the purpose of this new species? What motivates it? What does it do better than any other species?

   Yes, this is kind of silly. But it will allow you to view yourself through an entirely different lens. It will help you discover your true thoughts and motivations, which in turn will help you in coming up with your principles.

3) *Determine what is important.* The first thing you want to learn about yourself is what is truly important to you. Family? Spirituality? Duty to your country? Remember, look at yourself objectively. What have been your priorities in life? What have been your passions? Take some time to write down anything and everything that has been important to you.

   When you use an objective lens to write down what you have prioritized, you will likely feel both energized and ashamed by what you see. It will give you great insight into what has been important to you in the past and what you want to change in the future.

4) *Prioritize.* Now that you have everything that is important to you written down, you have probably noticed that you have a pretty long list. Mine was over twenty-five items long. There are lots of things that are important to who we are and who we want to become. But if you have twenty-five priorities, then you really have no priorities, so now it's time to determine what is really important to you. You need to determine the one thing that you will prioritize above all others.

   If you could choose just one thing to be important in your life, what would it be? Your family? Your religion? Your life's work? For me, it was willpower. It was my ultimate passion, the one thing I was extraordinarily good at, and I knew that if I could devote my life to strengthening my willpower, I would become better at everything else.

   Once you have found your top priority, move on to the second. If you could have only two priorities, what would they be? Then repeat the process for your top three priorities, your top four, and so on. There is no set number of priorities that you should have. The key is to have as few as possible while still having enough to become the person you want to be. Simply be mindful of when there seems to be a big drop-off in the importance of one priority to the next, and that will help you know when you've hit your number.

5) *Make a list of actionable principles.* Now that you have your priorities, it is time to put them into a list of actionable principles. To turn a priority into a principle, think about how that priority can be applied to a real-life situation where you will be tested.

For example, my second priority is "learning and growth." But "learning and growth" in itself is not a principle, so I had to think hard about how I could live up to that value in my daily life. I came up with the principle of "Become a better person today than I was yesterday," a clear statement that can be tested.

There is no requirement that you have one principle for every one priority. You may form two principles from one priority, or you may have two priorities that form one principle, and that's okay. Just continue working until you have a list of actionable principles that represents all your priorities. As with priorities, there is no set number of principles that is "best."

6) *Review and amend.* It is quite likely that whatever your starting list is, it will not be your final list. We all change our priorities as we get older, so set up a process to review and amend your principles. This could be an annual or biannual review in which you determine if you are still willing to fight for your principles. If you are not, then it might be time to make a change to your list.

Personally, at the end of every day I write down whether I have lived up to each of my principles. If I fail to live up to a certain principle too often, I take some time to reflect on whether I need to change myself or I need to change my principle. This process ensures that my principles are always up to date, and it also ensures that they are seen through my decisions and actions, rather than simply on a document on my computer or written in a notebook somewhere. No matter how admirable your list of principles is, it doesn't make a difference if people cannot see them through your actions. So make sure each one of them is up to date and that you are putting forth your best effort to live up to them every day.

Determining your list of principles is not only great for your personal growth and development, it is also great for your willpower. Having a list of principles that you strive to live by will give you the energy and motivation you need to overcome obstacles on your journey to greatness.

The most important thing is that the principles you come up with bring out the version of yourself that you truly want to become. Whether that is the greatest worker, the greatest writer, or the greatest parent, your principles should be a reflection of your unique ideals and values. You may not always live up to them, but you *will* be better for the effort.

Internal Locus of Control

Through his career, there were countless things that Lombardi could not control. He could not control the fact that he was Italian. He could not control the stereotypes that others held about Italians. He could not control which teams would see beyond his heritage and look at his results to know that he was the right man for the job. So to get through all of the struggles and not give up on his dream, he didn't focus on those things. He focused on what he *could* control.

With every job he took, he put forth the best effort he possibly could. He committed himself to learning more about the game and growing as a leader, even if he wasn't getting any respect for it in the form of a head coaching position. This focus is called the "internal locus of control," and it will help you persevere until you meet your goal—even if you're not getting the results you want right away.

No matter how hard you work, there will be factors outside of your control that affect how you reach your goal. Having an internal locus of control reminds you to expend your willpower working toward what you can control, while also letting go of the things you cannot. This will help you establish great behaviors that will eventually lead to the results you want.

To do this, you must shift your focus from being *results-oriented* to being *process-oriented*. If you are results-oriented, that means you focus all of your attention on the "after" photo. You focus on losing a certain amount of weight, getting a degree, winning a race, or reaching a sales target. And if you don't reach your end result, you fail. If you are process-oriented, on the other hand, that means you focus your attention on the journey. You focus on each healthy meal, each hour of studying, each run, and each sales call. And it is when you don't follow your process that you fail.

When you are focused on the result, each step of your journey seems insignificant—especially if the result is lofty. With each step toward your goal, you realize just how far away you are from achieving it. If you shift your focus to the process of taking each step perfectly, however, each step taken becomes a small win. You grow in confidence as you accumulate victories, and soon you realize you're pretty far down the road.

Becoming process-oriented will also help you respond better to failure. In those instances when things do not work out in your favor, you will naturally want to determine what went wrong. And because your primitive brain is evolved to avoid pain, it will look to blame outside factors for your failure—blame which probably isn't justified. If you do this, you will shut out your ability to learn from the mistakes you made.

If you shift your focus to the process and what you can control, however, you can learn from what went wrong and change it for next time. You can make constant tweaks and improvements because you are in control. Perhaps you tried to set up an exercise routine in the evenings, but had more post-work commitments than you thought you would. So you learn from that process and shift your exercise routine to the morning. You will be able to learn and grow from each step of the journey.

There are many advantages to creating goals. You gain focus, motivation, and confidence by setting goals and achieving them. But if you focus on results rather than the process, you can set yourself up to fail because you move the focus away from what you can control. There will always be outside factors that will influence the ultimate outcome of your efforts. But by shifting your focus to the process and factors within your control, you set yourself up to achieve small wins, to learn from experience, and to avoid trying to predict the future. Vince Lombardi was able to keep pushing until he achieved his dream because he wasn't focused on his results; he was focused on his effort.

Never-Ending Pursuit of Perfection

Despite his best intentions for perfection, Vince Lombardi knew what he was getting himself into when he began his job coaching the Packers. He had a losing team that was far from championship caliber. He wanted desperately to win every single game, but he didn't expect a championship. He didn't expect perfect results. Instead, he embarked on a never-ending pursuit of perfect process.

Just like there are aspects outside of your control that can affect your goals, aspects outside of the players' control can determine the final score of a football game. They might play perfect defense, but the opponent also might get in a few lucky bounces that are enough to win. They might get some bad calls at the worst possible times. And for whatever reason, a key player might simply be off his game enough to make the team lose—even if everyone else plays well. The team might play their hearts out and still end up walking away from the field defeated. Lombardi knew this, so instead of having his players focus on the scoreboard, he had them focus on their effort.

If there is only one thing you can control in life, it is your effort. With every decision you face, you alone decide how much energy you are willing to put into it. That holds true for working toward a goal, sticking to your principles, or even being a great member of your family. And that is why Lombardi's focus was not on reaching perfection, but in relentlessly chasing it.

Perfection is not found in results. Perfection is found in the process. It is in making sure that you do the right things to make progress every single day. That is the only thing you can control when working toward your dream. So as you move on from this book and begin implementing its ideas in your daily life, shift your idea of perfection from the result to the effort that it will take to get there. Then, when you inevitably reach your destination, you won't just have the life you've always wanted to live, you will become the person you have always wanted to be. But make sure you know the sacrifices that may come with that.

Sacrifices

The untold story of Vince Lombardi is the terrible toll his work took on his personal life. Throughout the course of his career, he spent as many waking hours as possible coaching. His mind was always on the team, the result from the last week, and their next opponent. His mind was so focused on the game, in fact, that sometimes he would get home from work and mistake his neighbor's house for his own.

As his wife Marie put it, "The beginning of the week he's very tense…I don't see him Monday, Tuesday, Wednesday at all. It must be very hard to do what he needs to do, and to do it alone."

His focus on football caused a lot of damage to Lombardi's family. Even when he was home, his mind was elsewhere. This made Marie feel incredibly lonely and caused her to turn to alcohol. She and their two children were forced to accept the fact that they were not as important to Lombardi as football was. Lombardi also had a mild bipolar disorder that went undiagnosed. They simply believed the reason he was a kind and gentle father on some days and an emotional wreck on others was due to the stress of his job. Today, his children can reflect on him with forgiveness, but during their childhood, they could not help but resent and fear him.

Deep down, Vince Lombardi truly wanted to do it all. He wanted to be a legendary football coach, a great husband, and a great father. But no person has the willpower to work sixteen stressful hours a day, six days a week, and be a truly great family man. So his wife and children suffered because of it.

Whatever greatness you seek, understand that it requires sacrifices. For Lombardi, that sacrifice was his family's happiness. You will probably not have to make as big of a sacrifice to accomplish what you want in life, but be sure you know what's truly at stake before you start your journey.

When you go through the exercise to determine your principles, make sure that you give great consideration to the prioritization section. It is crucial that you understand what is most important to you in life and are prepared to sacrifice the other things. The more focused you are, the more likely you will be to achieve Lombardi's level of greatness—but know the potential consequences. You do not have an endless supply of willpower. Trying to do it all is a sure recipe for disaster, so set your priorities and be prepared to make sacrifices.

Conclusion

Vince Lombardi was a football genius. But it was not his genius that made him a football legend; it was his willpower. Those who are unable to reach their dreams are not always the ones who fail. More often, it is those who stop pushing for great and settle for good. It is those who begin to compromise their principles and make decisions based on what others are doing. And it is those who give up because they are focused on their results, rather than their process.

On your journey to greatness, do not be tempted by the inevitable opportunities you will have to settle for the comfortable life that is easier and more practical. Fight for the great life that you know is possible. Determine the principles that will guide you, and never compromise them. Then, put all of your effort into reaching your destination, and prepare to embark on a never-ending pursuit of perfection.

Key Points

- *Don't settle for what's practical; work for what's possible.* Vince Lombardi had many opportunities to accept his fate as an assistant coach, but he didn't. He chose to keep fighting and earn his head-coaching dream. Most people never achieve greatness because at some point along the way they settle for the easier, more practical path. There is no shame in settling for a good life if that is what you truly want. But if you dream of more, do not lose sight of it.

- *Your principles will enhance your want power.* Having a set of guiding principles that reflect your morals, beliefs, and purpose will help give you the willpower to make tough decisions. Do not let outside pressure make you feel like there is something that *should* be one of your principles. If you do not genuinely believe in them, you won't see the benefits to your willpower.

• *Process-oriented goals are more effective than results-oriented goals.* Your results are ultimately out of your control. You may eat perfectly and exercise every day and still not lose ten pounds by a certain date. Your process, however, is within your control. You can control what you eat and how much you exercise. So focus your willpower on your process, and eventually you will achieve the results.

• *Greatness requires sacrifices.* You cannot have it all. Despite his iron will, Lombardi could not become both a legendary coach and a great father. Given his priorities, he probably should never have had a family. You likely won't have to make as big of a sacrifice, but understand that you may have to give up things you want for what you want most.

Strategies

1) *Determine your principles.* Take the time to discover what is most important to you.

2) *Focus on your process.* Change any results-oriented goals to process-oriented goals.

3) *Be honest about the sacrifice.* You cannot do it all. You have twenty-four hours in a day and a willpower muscle that can only take so much.

Chapter 11

The Next Generation

"My advice is: You always have to keep persevering."
– Temple Grandin

Temple Grandin's mother prayed for good news as she sent Temple to a speech therapist. Diagnosed with autism at the age of three, Temple was thought to be incapable of learning language. In the 1950s, that meant she would be institutionalized for her entire life unless she could show she was capable of entering school and learning with other children. Her parents had tried everything they could, and this speech therapist was their last resort.

Against all odds, young Temple made progress in speech therapy. It was slow, but after over a year she was able to speak well enough to be enrolled in a normal school. This was a huge win for Temple, but still her future seemed bleak.

She struggled throughout her entire school life because she simply did not think the way "normal" children did. She did not think in terms of words, only images. She struggled with empathy and did not understand basic human emotions or interactions. Her inability to relate to her peers and be understood by her teachers alienated Temple. She was constantly picked on, which led to problems with anxiety. Although she had overcome a huge obstacle in avoiding institutionalization, it appeared Temple would never be successful in mainstream society. She was just too different.

That started to change when Temple spent a summer living on her aunt's farm in Arizona. There, Temple was able to interact with her aunt's cattle and discover the deep connection she felt with them. Interacting with these animals felt right to her. For some reason, she felt a level of empathy for them that she could not feel for people.

Then Temple spotted a machine known as the "squeeze chute," which holds cattle tightly while they are examined, marked, or given veterinary treatment. Like all children, Temple had the desire to be hugged tightly to help her feel safe and secure. But she could not stand having another person hug her. It terrified her to be that vulnerable, and hugs would cause her to panic. When she saw the squeeze chute, however, she felt like this might give her the sensation she had been looking for—an embrace without vulnerability. So she used the squeeze chute on herself and instantly felt a sense of calm come over her. All her anxious feelings melted away, and she finally felt safe.

When she returned home from Arizona, Temple got straight to work on her second great passion in life: building things. She wanted to design and create a machine that would give her the same sensation she'd felt in the squeeze chute.

She was so passionate about this that she spent hours researching machine design. Because the purpose she was working for was so important to her, she forced herself to learn things through words. She fought through the frustration of reading and began teaching herself how to learn from a book. Eventually her frustration paid off, and she built a makeshift squeeze chute that could help calm her anxiety as she dealt with the social awkwardness of her adolescence.

After finishing her squeeze chute, Temple's curiosity only increased. She wanted to know why the machine impacted her so positively. So she became obsessed with how touch and pressure affect autistic children. Since she was still alienated from her peers, she had ample time for research and studying. It still took her much longer to read than it did other students, but it provided a great platform for her to develop her language skills. This helped her immensely as she progressed through high school, where learning from textbooks became increasingly important.

High school was still a struggle for Temple, but with each passing year, her options continued to grow. After years of research and remarkable improvements in her learning ability, Temple graduated high school and gained admission to Franklin Pierce University. After earning her bachelor's degree in psychology, Temple wanted to get back to what she was most passionate about: animals. So she went to Arizona State University to get her master's degree in animal science.

At Arizona State, she studied the design of feedlots and the behavioral responses of the animals in them. She, however, saw the designs completely differently than her peers and teachers. They seemed to not take the animals' thoughts or emotions into account at all; they were solely focused on how to make the design as efficient as possible.

Temple believed this was the key cause of the many animal deaths and injuries that tended to occur in the production process. Neither the animals nor their instincts were designed for life in a feedlot, so they would frighten, freeze, and panic under certain conditions. This had been completely overlooked by everyone else, and was what Temple was determined to fix.

After graduating, Temple began designing feedlots. She was determined to put an end to the pointless injuries and deaths. She knew that most of the problems came from cattle panicking, which frustrated workers, prompting them to force the cattle to move along, making their panic worse. Temple wanted to learn where and why the cattle were panicking in the first place. To do so, she went through the entire process from the cow's perspective, trying to see, think, and act like a cow.

Her empathy for cattle gave her a tremendous perspective from which to create her new feedlot design. She obsessed over each point and ensured that the cattle's psychological state was always cared for. She deliberately kept certain things out of their line of vision, ensured they would be able to keep their footing after falling down a ramp, and made certain their dip into water was so gentle that they didn't believe drowning was a possibility.

At first, slaughterhouse workers laughed at Temple for being so caring toward a group of animals that was just going to become someone's dinner anyway. But then they marveled at the new flow of the cattle as they happily walked through the process without being forced. The animals remained unbelievably calm, and there were hardly any pileups, injuries, or time lost in the process. It was incredible—and it could only have been accomplished by someone with a deep empathy for animals.

At one point, Temple had had no brighter future than to be one of the assembly-line workers in a slaughterhouse, but she wound up being perhaps the industry's greatest innovator.

Benefits of Adversity

From the time of her arrival in this world, Temple Grandin faced an uphill battle. At almost every step of her life, she was at a disadvantage. She could not talk properly, she could not learn properly, and she could not interact with others properly. It took remarkable willpower for her to overcome these challenges, but in the end, she actually benefitted from the adversity she faced.

Before she even entered school, Temple had already conquered the nearly impossible goal of learning to communicate. She may not have fully understood how important it was for her to enter school, but it was a huge win for her. She and her family now knew they could overcome extraordinary odds to help her achieve a normal life. So, although she had many challenges ahead of her, she now had the confidence in herself to overcome such hardships.

Then when she turned eleven, she had the luck to discover the cattle squeeze chute. When she used it on herself, the rush of calm she felt became the spark that would ignite her purpose in life. While her classmates' goals involved acquiring candy and baseball cards, Temple's were about learning how to build things and doing research on the effects of pressure on autistic children.

This purpose gave her so much want power that she could spend six hours at a time doing research—research that didn't just help her learn more about designing machines, but also helped her engage in the necessary deliberate practice of learning through words. She was focusing on her weaknesses, not her strengths. She was getting consistent feedback from her learning as she applied it to building the machine. And the process was highly repeatable as she spent hours reading, building, and tinkering.

So here we have a child who was born with a significant disadvantage in life, at a time when the best medical answer to her condition was institutionalization. Yet she not only attended school, she actually learned and grew faster intellectually than her peers, all the while growing more confident in her ability to overcome her weaknesses and achieve anything she set her mind to.

Self-Esteem

Starting in the 1970s, shortly after Temple's time in school, psychologists believed they had found the secret to success in the development of children: improving their self-esteem. It seemed so obvious. Study after study showed that those with the highest grades, the best health, the best jobs, and the most happiness all had high levels of self-esteem. So parents were encouraged to tell their children that they were exceptional, teachers were instructed to give check marks instead of grades, and coaches were told to give everyone a trophy.

However, psychologists created this self-esteem movement before conducting rigorous studies of whether high self-esteem was the *cause* of great success or the *result* of great success. Were kids with higher self-esteem really more likely to work harder? Or did kids with better work ethics, like Temple, simply earn a higher level of self-esteem through their efforts? Before truly knowing the answer to this question, psychologists bet on the former.

Sadly, they got it wrong. After studying an entire generation of children born into the self-esteem movement, researchers found no improvement in their grades, tendency toward alcohol and drug abuse, and obesity levels. Even worse, these children seem to be ill-prepared to handle adversity—simply avoiding it altogether or feeling terrible about themselves if they failed. The researchers were baffled. Boosting self-esteem was supposed to help children overcome challenges, not run away from them.

In order to see where they'd missed the mark, a group of researchers led by Donelson Forsyth took university students who'd recently received a C or below on their latest midterm exam and separated them into two groups. One group was given an encouraging message from the professor every week until the next exam. The messages contained praise of the students' intelligence and an expression of the belief that they were capable of much better than their last grade. The other group was given a neutral message where the professor didn't show any praise or belief in the students. The researchers believed that those who received praise and encouragement from the professor would use that boost to their self-esteem to motivate themselves. Then they would study harder and improve more on the next exam than the other group.

The results of the study, however, showed the exact opposite: The students who received an encouraging message from the professor did worse on the next exam than those who received a neutral message. And unfortunately, that wasn't the worst part. Those who were given praise and encouragement from the professor actually did worse on the next exam than they had on the midterm. Their scores dropped drastically, from an average of 59 percent down to 39 percent.

How could this be? How could the students actually perform worse after the boost in their self-esteem? In his book *Willpower*, Roy Baumeister concluded that by sending those encouraging messages, the professor made the students feel better about their own natural abilities. They began to believe that they were smarter than they actually were, so they spent even less time studying for the next exam because they felt it wasn't necessary.

Continuing studies have shown similar results. Time and time again, those considered "average performers" who receive boosts to their self-esteem do not improve; in fact, their performance actually gets worse. This phenomenon makes a lot of sense when considered through the lens of Temple Grandin. Throughout her early years of school, Temple had terrible self-esteem—social isolation will do that to a child—but as she continued to achieve small wins like getting into school, building machines, and teaching herself how to learn through words, she grew more confident. She learned that she could overcome obstacles, that she could get great results, and that she could even surpass her peers.

This gave her so much confidence, in fact, that she had the ability to enter the male-dominated slaughterhouse industry and propose radical ideas. A similar person who had received external boosts to her self-esteem all of her life would never have the confidence to do something like that. She would be so used to approval from others that the thought of failure would have been too great for her to want to take that risk. Temple, however, did not worry about the risk because she earned her feelings of self-worth through her own actions and accomplishments.

You probably don't want your children to have to endure the bullying that Temple Grandin did. Although you may know the advantages of adversity, you still want to keep your kids safe. So how can you instill in them the lessons from Temple Grandin without the torture? The answer comes from another study that began in the 1970s—with very different results.

The Marshmallow Test

The year was 1970, and psychologists Walter Mischel and Ebbe B. Ebbesen invited a group of four-year-olds into their laboratory for what was surely the toughest test of their short lives. They were put in a room by themselves with delicious, tempting marshmallows on plates in front of them. They were told that they could eat their marshmallows right away if they wanted to but that if they could wait fifteen minutes, they would earn a second marshmallow.

For a four-year-old, this was painful to say the least. Most of the children simply could not resist and ate their marshmallows right away. The ones who attempted to resist the temptation devised many coping strategies. They tried not looking at the marshmallow, covering their eyes, or turning around so that they could not see it. Others tried to distract themselves by kicking the desk, tugging on their pigtails, or stroking the marshmallow as if it were a tiny stuffed animal. Ultimately, less than one-third of the kids were able to resist the first marshmallow and earn the second.

This study was originally conducted to see at what age children begin to learn the benefits of delayed gratification. They conducted the same study with six-year-olds and found that they were indeed more successful in delaying gratification than the four-year-olds. These results proved that we learn the benefits of delaying gratification for larger rewards as we grow older. Test completed—or so they thought.

The researchers conducted a follow-up study involving the original group of four-year-olds once they became adolescents. Interestingly, the ones who had been able to wait for the second marshmallow were described by parents and teachers as significantly more competent than those who'd been unable to wait. A few years later, further studies showed that those self-disciplined kids also scored higher on the SAT than their impatient counterparts.

Continuing studies showed that those kids beat their counterparts on nearly all measures of life success. They achieved more academically, had higher incomes and better health, and reported greater satisfaction in their lives. The ability to wait for a second marshmallow as a four-year-old proved to be a better predictor of success than almost every other factor, including IQ, quality of education, and family income. Those who had the willpower to earn a marshmallow at age four also had the willpower to earn great grades, a great job, and a great life.

Over the last forty years, psychologists have repeated this study with similar results. For some reason, the ability to delay the immediate gratification of a marshmallow as a four-year-old means that you will also be able to delay the immediate gratification of video games in favor of doing homework. You will be able to delay the immediate gratification of living above your means in favor of investing your money wisely. And you will be able to delay the gratification of short-term indulgences in favor of long-term health.

So what was it that was special about these four-year-olds? Could it be that these kids, and all of the heroes in this book for that matter, were simply born with more willpower than others? The answer is a resounding no! It turned out that the successful four-year-olds were actually raised in a very different environment than the others who were not able to resist the temptation of the marshmallow. At a time when parenting books were promoting the value of self-esteem, the successful children were learning the value of self-control.

They had to do more chores than the other children. They were given praise and rewards only when they earned them by behaving well and getting good grades in school. Rather than simply giving their children a trophy, the parents of these four-year-olds made them work for it.

As you have learned throughout this book, success does not come from innate gifts or privileges. World-class athletes, brilliant scientists, and successful businesspeople were not born with more talent than others. And so it should not shock you that things like family income, neighborhood status, and school quality are not the most important factors in developing successful children. While each of these factors does play a role in children's development, the marshmallow test shows that they can have less of an impact if children develop strong self-control.

Developing Willpower for Your Children

To achieve anything great in life, your children must face some adversity. No matter how much money your family has or how naturally gifted your children are, they will have to deal with setbacks. They will have to give up what they want now for what they want most later, and they will have to put in hours and hours of practice in their domain. All of these things require strong willpower, and children who grow up practicing self-control have a willpower advantage over others, regardless of talent or privilege.

Here are some exercises you can use to help your kids develop their willpower:

1) *Give them chores.* Chores are the easiest and most effective way for children to develop their willpower. Chores are inherently boring for most kids, so doing them forces children to develop their willpower, especially when they would rather be playing video games, watching TV, or hanging out with friends.

There are a few key points to keep in mind when giving your children chores; the first is to have your child do chores even if you need to completely redo them later. A five-year-old probably will not do the best job of cleaning the bathroom. He will miss spots, he won't be able to reach everywhere, and he simply will not know what quality cleaning is. But you are not having him do chores to make less work for you. You're having him do chores to help strengthen his willpower and build his confidence. It's not about the clean bathroom; it's about the development of the child's willpower.

The second thing to keep in mind is to reward your children for doing their chores. Some parents are extremely worried about paying their children for doing things they're "supposed to do." But getting rewards for hard work is what life is all about. If you work hard in society, you earn the things that you want. Rewarding your children for doing their chores teaches them that there is value in working hard.

2) *Have them make their beds.* Making the bed is another simple way to improve children's willpower. To children, making the bed seems somewhat pointless. They are probably the only ones who are going to see their beds, so what does it matter? But an untidy bed leads to an untidy room, which can actually lead to lower willpower.

A made bed, by contrast, means that children start each day with a small win. They get a sense of earned accomplishment and well-being that can lead to even more victories throughout the day. It may not seem like a big deal—and that is precisely the point. By teaching them the importance of getting this small detail right on a daily basis, they will learn to focus on getting other small details right in their lives as well. Over time, this will have profound effects on their success in other, non-related areas of their lives.

3) *Preach large, long-term rewards.* As Baumeister and Tierney point out in their book, one of the most successful cultures when it comes to raising disciplined children is the Asian culture. Rather than offering praise and encouraging self-esteem in their children, Asians preach discipline and earning long-term rewards. This has led Asian-American students on average to outperform all other cultures academically, and part

of the reason for that is their parents offering large rewards for long-term achievements.

It is hard to stay focused on a long-term goal when there is not a clear connection between the goal and your work today. It requires willpower to stay on track and not lose sight of what you are working for. Offering a large long-term reward for achieving a long-term goal helps children practice giving up short-term pleasures in favor of working for a greater purpose. Not only will they then achieve big things, but they will also strengthen their willpower in the process.

4) *Be consistent.* You will have many low-willpower days on which accomplishing your own goals will be hard, and making sure your kids accomplish theirs will be even harder. On those days, you will be tempted to do their chores yourself or turn a blind eye to an unmade bed. But consistency is just as important for your child's willpower as it is for your own. So ensure you stay on top of them—even on the hardest days.

Being consistent also means adhering yourself to the rules you set for your children. If you tell them to make their beds, make sure yours is made as well. If you tell them the value of large long-term rewards, make sure you're sharing how you're working toward yours, too. Kids respond best to a consistent, honest message—whether through words or actions.

Doing chores, making the bed, and working for long-term rewards helps kids develop willpower to take on other challenges, like studying, homework, and extracurricular activities. Over time, they gain skills, knowledge, and confidence from these activities that lead them to success in adult life as well. Developing willpower is far from easy, but the marshmallow test proves that it will be worth it—for you, and for your children. And as they begin to strengthen their willpower and earn their confidence, you can help them get to the next level by following the advice of one of the greatest leaders of young people the world has ever known.

Praise Effort, Not Results

The clock was ticking down as the UCLA Bruins were about to defeat the Seattle University Redhawks in the Round of 16 game of the 1964 NCAA basketball tournament. The Bruins had come into the game undefeated and were up ninety-five to ninety. Their win was all but assured, but legendary basketball coach John Wooden was not happy. His team had underestimated the tenacity of the Redhawks. UCLA had come into the game expecting to win with ease and did not play with great effort and focus. They had taken it easy on defense and allowed the Redhawks to score almost at will.

Luckily, the Bruins hit enough shots to outscore the Redhawks and win the game. Wooden, however, knew that if his team showed this same type of effort on defense against better competition in the final rounds of the tournament, they were destined to lose. So despite the victory, Wooden scolded his team. He demanded of them greater effort, focus, and resiliency. He demanded that they play up to their potential—or their undefeated season would be a waste.

The team responded well, winning their next three games without giving up more than eighty-four points against much better opposition than the Redhawks. This led the Bruins to finish the season undefeated and win their first of ten NCAA Championships under Wooden over the next twelve years.

What is the lesson here? That being harsh is the key to raising successful kids? No. Wooden may have seemed to be tough with his players in the game against the Redhawks, but what he was really doing was getting them to focus on their effort, not their results. Despite all of his success as a basketball coach, Wooden claimed that he never once cared what the final score of the game was. Like Lombardi, what he cared about was whether they played with great effort.

As a result, there were some games where his team won yet he was not happy, and there were other games where they lost and he was extremely proud. He knew that aspects outside of your control can determine the final score of a basketball game; you may play your heart out and end up walking away from the court defeated. Knowing that, Wooden chose to praise his players based on their effort instead of praising them based on the scoreboard. And that is how he brought the best out of his players every day.

When your child is trying to achieve something—whether it's a grade in school or getting a spot on a sports team—there is a basic formula that comes into play:

Child's talent + Child's effort = Child's result

The big mistake that parents make is praising their children based only on their talents and their results. This usually involves saying something like, "You're so smart; I know you can do it!" and then praising the end result no matter what. This type of praise teaches kids the wrong lesson. It reinforces the message that talent is the most important factor in achieving great results and that your results should be praised regardless of the amount of effort you put forth.

This would be like Kobe Bryant's parents telling him that he had a remarkable talent for basketball before he entered basketball camp as a twelve-year-old and then, even though he did not score a single point, awarding him a trophy at the end of the camp out of fear that his failure would damage his self-esteem. Sure, that might have made Kobe feel better about his experience and skills, but it would not have allowed him to feel the pain of failure, acknowledge the reality of his situation, and learn a valuable lesson from the experience.

Luckily, his parents didn't adhere to the teachings of the self-esteem movement. Instead, they allowed their son to confront the feeling of failure. Then, through the story of Michael Jordan, they taught him that failure isn't final. They allowed him to see with his own eyes that failure can be overcome with effort. They let Kobe earn his confidence as he got progressively better through practice, eventually achieving greatness.

It is tempting to build up your children's confidence by praising their natural abilities and sheltering them from failure. It is not easy to instill the value of effort in them when they cannot fully grasp how that effort will benefit them in the long term. That is why most parents choose the easy route. They choose to call their children brilliant, and mask any poor results by giving them a trophy for simply showing up.

You must fight against this temptation. You must teach your children that not everyone is great at something right away—and that that is okay. They may not be the smartest kids in school, the best singers in the choir, or the most talented players at a basketball camp, but that does not mean they should give up.

Nobody wants his kids to fail, but failure is a part of life. All of the heroes you've read about in this book have failed at something. But it was their failures that motivated them to outwork everyone around them so they wouldn't feel that pain again. Failing is tough. It hurts the self-esteem. But if your child learns how to deal with failure, it will give her the confidence to take risks, learn from mistakes, and persevere—all of the traits that we wanted to instill in our children through the self-esteem movement.

I hope that I have now convinced you that at their young age, your children's results are irrelevant. Being great at something now is not as important as developing the willpower needed to become great at something later. Temple Grandin couldn't read until she was twelve, J.K. Rowling didn't have a book published until she was twenty-eight, and Vince Lombardi didn't have a chance to be a head coach until he was forty-six. These people were not child prodigies. Their results at an early age were not spectacular. What made them all great was the fact that they didn't quit. They gave their best efforts every day, until finally they achieved their remarkable results. And that drive for effort and perseverance is what you must instill in your children if you want them to be successful.

Conclusion

Temple Grandin was dealt a terrible hand in life. She was born with a severe affliction that left many to languish in institutions. But she was able to achieve small win after small win and develop the willpower to take on bigger and bigger challenges as she grew older. This goes against what we have been telling parents for years about raising children with high levels of self-esteem. Those with an inflated self-esteem are rarely given the chance to face adversity, and therefore do not get the opportunity to earn their confidence and develop their willpower.

For the sake of your children, avoid the temptation to make things easy for them. Allow them to learn the value of hard work, develop their willpower, and deal with failure, because if they can do that when they're young, they will be much happier and more successful in their adult lives.

Key Points

- *There is a downside to the self-esteem movement.* When adults artificially boost children's self-esteem, those children begin to overvalue their talent and undervalue their effort in achieving results. Later in life, this causes them to give up something if they feel they have no natural gift for it.

- *Instead of boosting self-esteem, boost self-control.* The marshmallow test proves the value of having children with high self-control. These children also had high levels of self-esteem, but they earned that through setting long-term goals and working hard to achieve them.

- *Praise effort, not results.* At a young age, a child's results are irrelevant. What is much more important is learning the value of effort. Any child can begin strengthening his willpower, but he first needs to understand why it's important. So praise children based for their effort, not their results.

Strategies

1) *Give children chores to do (especially making the bed).* Chores aren't fun for kids, so it takes willpower to get them done. The more they strengthen their willpower muscle now, the stronger it will be later.

2) *Give them a large long-term reward for hard work.* No matter how young your child, providing a large reward for long-term hard work will teach her that hard work pays if you can stick with it.

3) *Keep it consistent.* Ensure your children stick with their willpower workouts every day. As with all you have learned about willpower, consistency beats intensity.

Chapter 12

The Journey without an End

"I wake up every day wanting to change the world. Every day."
– Alex Kleiner

It seemed to be the party that would never end. The Internet boom of the 1990s brought with it unheard-of opportunities for advancements in technology, communication, and entrepreneurship. The costs of starting a new business were lower than ever, and the potential profits were unlimited. So brilliant entrepreneurial minds from all over the world started new businesses with hopes of building the next great technology company. Among them was Frictionless Commerce, a business-to-consumer startup that created comparison-shopping technology for online shoppers.

With two of his fellow MIT graduate students, and another founder who would join later, Alex Kleiner started Frictionless in 1998 at the height of the dot-com bubble. As the founding CEO, Alex raised nine million dollars from investors, signed high-profile clients, and was responsible for leading the team to more than two million dollars in revenue in the company's first two years.

As a first-time CEO, Alex needed to learn how to manage rapid growth at a time when growth meant more than any other metric. It was hardly an easy process, but unlike other start-up CEOs at the time, Alex was never in it for the money. He was in it to make an intrinsic difference.

"I wake up every day wanting to change the world," he said. "Take the handful that you are given and leave an armful for those that follow." This attitude of leaving the world a better place was manifested in the business results of Frictionless, as the company didn't lose a single client during their first year and a half.

But in 2000, the technology world woke up to the brutal reality that there was a bubble about to burst. There were thousands of terrible Internet companies and millions of dollars in projected revenues that would never become a reality. Companies failed. Then the companies that serviced those companies failed. Then investors pulled their money out of the remaining companies as fast as they could before those companies also failed. Some of the hottest start-ups were now worth nothing more than the value of their domain name. The party was over.

But as the rest of the technology start-up CEOs woke up in a panic, Alex still woke up with a purpose. Times were going to be hard, but he and the whole Frictionless team were going to persevere.

The Frictionless Commerce team confronted the difficult facts. They had to learn where they fit within this new economy. Once they determined that they needed to completely change their business model to survive, they began to reinvent themselves. The team worked relentlessly to be able to count themselves among the few start-ups that would come out of the bubble-burst alive. This involved completely changing their business model to target the business-to-business market. It was hard work, but the change looked promising as they secured some of the largest companies in the world as customers. Step by step, they navigated through the hostile market, until after over five years of tireless work, Frictionless emerged from the crash even stronger than it had been before and was acquired by SAP for fifty million dollars. And the platform that was developed by Frictionless Commerce is still in use today at hundreds of large organizations around the globe.

How Heroes Respond to Failure

Frictionless Commerce was destined to fail. Their business model simply would not survive in the new reality of the marketplace. But Alex and his team responded to their failed business model by confronting the situation and persevering, just like every other hero in this book.

When he was twelve years old, Kobe Bryant showed little promise in basketball and was about to give up the sport forever. When she was twenty-eight years old, J.K. Rowling hit rock bottom and was living as a single mother on welfare. When he was thirty years old, Steve Jobs was incredibly reckless and was kicked out of the company he'd created.

You have seen this theme throughout this book: A hero gave everything he or she had in pursuit of his or her dream, but it wasn't enough. He used all of his passion. She used all of her strength. They both used all of their willpower. Yet they needed something more. They needed to keep going.

Whether it was Tim Grover being rejected by the Chicago Bulls, Joe De Sena being told by doctors he would never run again, or Vince Lombardi being rejected by dozens of teams for a position as head coach; those heroes fought, and those heroes lost. But their failure was never the end of their stories—and that is what is different about them.

While Alex Kleiner and the Frictionless team were scrambling to reinvent their start-up to survive the burst of the dot-com bubble, there were countless others who simply accepted their fate. They gave up, they settled, and they never made their dreams a reality.

The heroes I researched had lots of chances to do the same. They were defeated and could have easily ended their journey to greatness, but they didn't. They kept going. They persevered.

Overcoming Defeat

After spending five years living as a single mother in poverty, J.K. Rowling finally completed *Harry Potter and the Philosopher's Stone*. Unfortunately, publishers at the time didn't love Harry as much as the rest of the world soon would. Rowling and her agent were rejected by the first publisher they sent the book to, then the next...and the next. The first twelve publishers Rowling sent the book to rejected it.

Imagine the pain of pouring every ounce of your strength into something for five years, and being told it was no good. Not just by one person, or two, but by *twelve*. Many authors in her position would, and have, given up—but Rowling was not fazed. She kept pushing. And the thirteenth publisher finally said "yes."

Every hero in this book faced a similar failure at some point in his or her life. And every one also chose not to quit. They used their failures as motivation to push even harder to come out victorious the next time.

At some point in your life, you are going to lose a battle. You are going to fight with every ounce of strength you have, and you are still going to lose. But what defines your character is that after you lose that battle, you do not lose yourself. You do not compromise your principles. You do not stop fighting for what you really want in life. And you still wake up every day with a purpose.

Failure isn't final. You might not reach a goal on the first, second, or even twelfth attempt. But you will never truly lose until you stop trying. Until you finally throw in the towel, there is always hope. All you need to do is get up one more time than you've been knocked down.

Refusing to Settle

When Steve Jobs was kicked out of Apple Computer in 1985, he could have taken his hundred-million-dollar fortune and retired to a life of luxury and relaxation. And who would have blamed him? That's more money than most of us ever dream of having. So why bother doing anything else?

Thankfully, Jobs didn't think like that. He got right back to work starting a new company, NeXT. Then he saved a struggling digital animation company, Pixar. Then he came back to reinvent his former company, Apple.

Imagine where the world would be today if Steve Jobs had settled. Think about all of the joy that Pixar's movies have brought to children. Think about the revolutions in computers, phones, and even the music industry that have taken place because of what Apple did under his leadership.

The desire to quit doesn't always come from failure; it often comes from settling for "good enough." For most of us, that settling takes the form of "practicality." It is practical to stop pushing, to not take risks, and to give up what you truly want in life for what is comfortable and safe. Now, there is no shame in settling for a comfortable, practical life if that is what you truly want. But be honest with yourself; if you dream of more, do not lose sight of it. Perseverance isn't just about refusing to quit; it's also about refusing to settle.

Embracing a Journey without an End

Hello Colin,
I just signed up for your course. Looking forward to reviewing it. All the best.
Alex

Almost ten years after Frictionless was sold for fifty million dollars, Alex Kleiner sent me that message. He was one of the students in my first course on the science of willpower. He'd already graduated from MIT, raised nine million dollars to found a company, and helped lead that company through one of the hardest economic environments to a successful acquisition. Yet he was still looking to strengthen his willpower and continue to grow. Why? Because Alex, like all the other heroes, is on a journey without an end.

After he sold his company, Alex continued learning, growing as a leader, and waking up with a purpose. He is now with one of the fastest growing technology companies in Silicon Valley. In 2011, he was hired as the first person on the ground in Europe in order to establish an overseas presence. Alex started with nothing more than a phone, a laptop, and a will to change the world. Just four years later, the company was recognized for disrupting their market space and was named "Hottest Emerging B2B Software Business in Europe," over several public companies worth billions of dollars.

Even when heroes succeed in their quests, they still persevere, because achieving greatness is not a destination—it is a journey. I hope this book will help you achieve your purpose, but in order to do that, you must embrace the truth that achieving any goal is simply a pit stop on your quest. Once you reach it, there will always be another goal, another challenge, and another destination worth fighting for. And that is what achieving greatness is all about.

Conclusion

There is no secret to success in life. I have learned a lot from my research about what it takes to become truly great at something, and the biggest lesson is that, above all else, you must have the willpower to persevere. Those who reach greatness are simply the ones who were able to roll with the punches and keep moving forward, no matter what.

In your life, you will lose, you will fail, and you will be tempted to settle for "good enough." But if you can keep going, if you can keep pushing, and if you can will yourself to get up just one more time than you are knocked down, eventually you will achieve greatness—no matter how long it takes.

Key Points

- *Every person fails, but every hero perseveres.* There is no way to avoid failure in life. Those who reach greatness aren't the ones who avoid failure. They're the ones who persevere through it.

- *Perseverance means not accepting defeat, not settling for "good enough," and never ending your journey.* When J.K. Rowling was rejected by publishers, she didn't accept defeat. When Steve Jobs could have retired with a fortune, he refused the idea of settling. And after Alex Kleiner sold his startup for millions, he still woke up with a purpose to change the world.

Strategies

1) When you face fear, failure, or the temptation to settle, think about one of these heroes—and never give up.

Epilogue

How This Book Became a Reality

It was a beautiful Saturday in early September, and I was in total bliss. I was at a lake house just north of my home in Chicago, and people I loved surrounded me. We were simply relaxing and enjoying the last days of summer. But as I looked out at the sun setting over the lake, a sudden rush of panic came over me. This was all a lie. In reality, I was doomed.

The journey to that moment began years earlier when I first became curious about what exactly separated the world's greatest successes from everyone else. I've been a hero-worshipper all of my life. I put posters of athletes, movie stars, and great leaders in my room as a kid and dreamed of becoming just like them. Then as I grew older, I wanted to do more than just dream—I wanted to understand.

I began to read the biographies of some of my greatest heroes. The list included Arnold Schwarzenegger, Steve Jobs, J.K. Rowling, and many others who achieved true greatness in their fields. As I read about each hero, I tried to understand what it was exactly that made them different. Was it just luck that catapulted them to the top? Or was there some trait that they all had in common that I could learn from?

I found things that were pretty obvious indicators of success—dreaming big, setting goals, working hard, and so on. But these alone could not be the answer I was looking for. After all, there are millions of dreamers, goal-setters, and hard workers out there who don't become a billionaire author or a bodybuilding champion. So what was the difference?

After pondering the answer to that question for a long time, I came across something called "the science of willpower" in a chapter of Charles Duhigg's book *The Power of Habit*. As I read through it, I began to feel a rush of excitement I couldn't put into words. This was the answer I'd been looking for.

I immediately searched for every book on the subject I could get my hands on. After devouring those, I was still hungry for more. So I began reading what many would consider dry, boring scientific studies without any loss of enthusiasm. Every day I was learning more about how willpower works and seeing how each concept I learned about was used by my heroes—whether they understood the science or not.

For years, though, this was merely a personal curiosity. I simply learned the science, applied it to my life, and enjoyed the benefits. I was able to stop eating junk food and start eating healthy. I was able to go from not working out at all to being an elite athlete. I was able to overcome my fear of vulnerability and begin networking with others. Ultimately, I was able to set my mind to something and stick with it until it was done.

Then I realized that what I learned from my research was too important to keep to myself—I had to begin sharing it with the world. So I left my steady, well-paid job to dedicate myself full time to researching and writing about the science of willpower on a site I created called "Willpowered."

The site was far from an instant hit, but after six months of writing every day, it was clear that I was onto something. Thousands of people from all over the world were now visiting the site and e-mailing me about how my work was improving their lives. This was enough progress to get investors on board, get office space, and get interns to help. The future was bright, and I couldn't wait to reach even more people around the world.

Things continued to look promising. We had thousands of daily visitors, many online students, and the site was growing—but not enough to be sustainable. After another five months,

Willpowered was still operating at a loss and showing few signs of improvement. That's when I took my fateful trip to the lake house and woke up to the reality of the situation. In just forty-five days, I would be out of cash and forced to shut down the site.

I spent the rest of the weekend letting the emotions wash over me. *I'm just one of the millions of writers who aren't able to turn their work into a living. I'm just going to be a statistic among the 90 percent of businesses that fail. My dream of sharing the science of willpower with the world is going to die. How could I let this happen?*

Then I realized that I still didn't truly understand the willpower of my heroes, because I had not yet had this moment: the moment when Arnold Schwarzenegger was sent to the military, the moment when Joe De Sena was told he would never run again, or the moment when Tim Grover had to persuade Michael Jordan after already being told "no." In this moment, you have two choices: to accept defeat, or to fight back with strength you didn't even know you had. Every hero I researched had had this moment at some point their lives and came out victorious. It was time to see if I could as well. *I still have forty-five days left*, I thought. *This isn't over. It's time to get to work.*

After that trip came some of the hardest days of my life. I worked from the moment I woke up until the moment I went to bed. I was in a constant battle with doubt and fear as I pushed my comfort zone on a daily basis. I was flat-out exhausted, and I needed to use every ounce of mental strength I had.

But when I felt like I was going through hell, I reframed my perspective by thinking about how much better my situation was than Joe De Sena's when he was nearly freezing to death in Canada. I ate only low-glycemic foods and ensured I got the most willpower out of every hour of sleep I was able to get. I meditated to strengthen my willpower, stayed focus on my goal, and pushed my comfort zone daily. And above all else, I increased my want power by remembering the purpose of sharing the lessons in this book. In the end, I was victorious. I saved the company and *The Will of Heroes* became a reality.

I'm telling you this story because I didn't just write about the concepts in this book—I live them. I use them when all is going well and I simply want to add a new routine to my life, or when everything seems hopeless and I need to make a miracle happen. So whether you picked up this book because you want to make major changes, or you simply want to be a little more disciplined in your daily life, I am confident that by implementing the strategies you have learned here, you will achieve whatever greatness you seek.

Acknowledgements

I owe a debt of gratitude to people all over the world for their help in bringing this book to life.

I thank my parents for their endless support and understanding of my desire to follow an unconventional path. I thank my girlfriend, Jackie McDermott, for her undying faith in me and for helping me get through some tough experiences.

I thank Brianna Schmall for designing the book cover, and Sarah Dawson for her terrific job editing the manuscript. I thank Jeffrey Harrington for his mentorship and guidance, Chris Paredes for providing critical feedback and suggestions, and Owen Brittan for holding me accountable to finish what I started.

I thank Roy Baumeister for his pioneering research, and John Tierney for co-authoring their excellent book, *Willpower.* I thank Kelly McGonigal for her brilliant ideas in *The Willpower Instinct,* Robert Greene for his inspirational stories in *Mastery,* Geoff Colvin for his explanation of deliberate practice in *Talent is Overrated,* and the countless other authors and researchers whose work helped to form the ideas in this book.

I thank Kobe Bryant, Wolfgang Amadeus Mozart, Joe De Sena, Tim Grover, David Blaine, Arnold Schwarzenegger, J.K. Rowling, Steve Jobs, Jure Robic, Warren Buffett, Vince Lombardi, and Temple Grandin for inspiring me to follow a path to greatness.

I thank Alex Kleiner for sharing his story and for his help in bringing *The Will of Heroes* to life. I thank Alex Semenov for his business advice and for his generous support in publishing this book. Finally, I thank all of my friends, family, colleagues, and subscribers from all over the world for pledging their support *for*

The Will of Heroes on Kickstarter. Raising the money to fund this book was one of the proudest moments of my life, and I will be forever grateful to all of you.

Bibliography

Introduction: The Power of Will

Kobe Bryant basketball camp story: Bryant, K. (2014, December 15). Zero | by Kobe Bryant. http://www.theplayerstribune.com/kobe-passes-jordan/

Examples of Bryant's work ethic: Manfred, T. (2013, August 9). 17 Examples Of Kobe Bryant's Insane Work Ethic.

Chapter 1: The Myth of Talent

The Wolfgang Amadeus Mozart story: Melograni, P., & Cochrane, L. (2007). *Wolfgang Amadeus Mozart: A biography.* Chicago: University of Chicago Press.

Inferences about Mozart and the role of talent: Greene, R. (2012). *Mastery.* New York: Viking; Colvin, G. (2008). *Talent is overrated: What really separates world-class performers from everybody else.* New York: Portfolio.

The discovery of the ten-year rule: Hayes, J. (1990). Cognitive Processes in Creativity. *Handbook of Creativity,* 135-145.

Study of deliberate practice: Ericsson, K. A., Krampe, R. T., & Tesch-Römer, C. (1993). The role of deliberate practice in the acquisition of expert performance. *Psychological Review,* 100(3), 363-406.

The 10,000-hour rule: Gladwell, M. (2008). *Outliers: Why some people succeed and some don't.* New York: Little Brown & Co. & Greene R. (2012). Mastery. New York: Viking.

Deliberate practice example of two players shooting baskets: Expert Performance: Apologies to Dr. Ericsson, but it is not 10,000 hours of deliberate practice - Aubrey Daniels' Blog. (2009). http://aubreydaniels.com/blog/2009/07/21/expert-performance-apologies-to-dr-ericsson-but-it-is-not-10000-hours-of-deliberate-practice/

Characteristics of deliberate practice: Colvin, G. (2008). *Talent is overrated: What really separates world-class performers from everybody else.* New York: Portfolio.

Chapter 2: Understanding Willpower

Joe De Sena story: De Sena, J., & O'Connell, J. (2014). *Spartan up!: A take-no-prisoners guide to overcoming obstacles and achieving peak performance in life.* Houghton Mifflin Harcourt.

Triathlon story: Helm, B. (2014, April 21). Joe De Sena's Spartan Empire. http://www.mensjournal.com/adventure/races-sports/joe-de-senas-spartan-empire-20140421

Cookies and radishes study: Baumeister, R. F., Bratslavsky, E., Muraven, M., & Tice, D. M. (1998). Ego depletion: Is the active self a limited resource? *Journal of Personality and Social Psychology,* 74(5), 1252-1265.

Idea of the primitive brain and the modern brain: McGonigal, K. (2012). *The willpower instinct: How self-control works, why it matters, and what you can do to get more of it.* New York: Avery.

The motivations of the limbic system (primitive brain): Wise, R. (2002). Brain Reward Circuitry. *Neuron* 36.2: 229-40.

How socialization evolved our brain: Dunbar, R. (2003). THE SOCIAL BRAIN: Mind, Language, And Society In Evolutionary Perspective. *Annual Review of Anthropology,* 163-181.

The function of the prefrontal cortex (modern brain): Irwin, L. (1988). *Comparative Neuroscience and Neurobiology.* Boston: Birkhäuser.

Categories of willpower: McGonigal, K. (2012). *The willpower instinct: How self-control works, why it matters, and what you can do to get more of it.* New York: Avery.

"I don't" strategy: Patrick, V., & Hagtvedt, H. (2012) "I Don't" versus "I Can't": When Empowered Refusal Motivates Goal-Directed Behavior. *Journal of Consumer Research* 39.2: 371-81.

"Get to" strategy: Clear, J. (2013) How to Be Thankful For Your Life by Changing Just One Word. http://jamesclear.com/how-to-be-thankful

How your perspective affects your willpower: Job, V., Dweck, C. & Walton, G. (2010) Ego Depletion--Is It All in Your Head?: Implicit Theories About Willpower Affect Self-Regulation. *Psychological Science* 21.11 1686-693. Web.

Chapter 3: Fueling Your Willpower

Tim Grover story: Grover, T., & Wenk, S. (2014). *Relentless: From good to great to unstoppable.* Simon and Schuster.

Tim Grover conversation with athlete and diet plan: Grover, T. (Nov. 25, 2014). Tim Grover debunks the business of "Healthy

Eating." http://www.si.com/edge/2014/11/24/the-business-of-healthy-eating.

The effects of glucose on willpower: Baumeister, R. & Tierneym J. (2011) *Willpower: Rediscovering the Greatest Human Strength.* New York: Penguin.

The willpower fuel: Gailliot, M. T., Baumeister, R. F., Dewall, C. N., Maner, J. K., Plant, E. A., Tice, D. M., . . . Schmeichel, B. J. (2007). Self-control relies on glucose as a limited energy source: Willpower is more than a metaphor. *Journal of Personality and Social Psychology, 92*(2), 325-336.

Good glucose and bad glucose: Gailliot, M., & Baumeister, R. (2007). The Physiology Of Willpower: Linking Blood Glucose To Self-Control. *Personality and Social Psychology Review,* 303-327.

Low-glycemic food list: Pollan, M. (2009) *Food Rules: An Eater's Manual.* New York: Penguin.

Why we get cravings: Olds, J., & Milner, P. (1953). Positive Reinforcement Produced By Electrical Stimulation Of Septal Area And Other Regions Of Rat Brain. *Journal of Comparative and Physiological Psychology,* 419-427.

The story of desire in the Stone Age: McGonigal, K. (2012). *The willpower instinct: How self-control works, why it matters, and what you can do to get more of it.* New York: Avery.

Pause and take five deep breaths strategy: Segerstrom, S., Hardy, J., Evans, D., Winters, N. Pause and plan: Self-regulation and the heart. Washington, DC, *US: American Psychological Association,* xiv, 181-198.

Positive procrastination strategy: Mcclure, S., Ericson, K., Laibson, D., Loewenstein, G., & Cohen, J. (2007). Time Discounting for Primary Rewards. *Journal of Neuroscience*, 5796-5804.

Don't feel guilty strategy: Adams, C., & Leary, M. (2007). Promoting Self–Compassionate Attitudes Toward Eating Among Restrictive and Guilty Eaters. *Journal of Social and Clinical Psychology*, 26(10), 1120-1144.

Your willpower is strongest in the morning: Baumeister, R. F., Bratslavsky, E., Muraven, M., & Tice, D. M. (1998). Ego depletion: Is the active self a limited resource? *Journal of Personality and Social Psychology*, 74(5), 1252-1265.

Value of small wins: Duhigg, C. (2012). *The power of habit: Why we do what we do in life and business.* New York: Random House; Bandura, A., & Schunk, D. (1981). Cultivating Competence, Self-Efficacy, and Intrinsic Interest Through Proximal Self-Motivation. *Journal of Personality and Social Psychology*, 586-598.

Connections of sleep and exercise to willpower: McGonigal, K. (2012) *The Willpower Instinct: How Self-Control Works, Why It Matters, and What You Can Do to Get More of It.* New York: Avery.

Sleep and willpower: Spiegel, K., Tasali, E., Leproult, R., & Van Cauter, E. (2009). Effects Of Poor And Short Sleep On Glucose Metabolism And Obesity Risk. *Nature Reviews Endocrinology*, 253-261.

Mild prefrontal disfunction: Kilgore, W., Kahn-Green, E., Lipizzi, E., Newman, R., Kamimori, G. & Balkin, J (2008). Sleep deprivation reduces perceived emotional intelligence and constructive thinking skills. *Sleep Medicine.* 517-526.

Involuntary sleep statistic: Morbidity and Mortality Report (Vol. 60, No. 8) Centers for Disease Control.

Meditation and willpower: Mahoney, C. R., & Lieberman, H. R. (2012). Nutritional countermeasures for cognitive performance decrements following sleep deprivation. *Sleep Deprivation, Stimulant Medications, and Cognition,* 199-208.

Value of a completely dark room: Dijk, D., & Archer, S. (2009). Light, Sleep, and Circadian Rhythms: Together Again. *PLoS Biology,* E1000145-E1000145.

Value of napping: Feature, J (29 Nov. 2011) WebMD Magazine. Power Naps: Napping Benefits, Length, and Tips. *WebMD.*

Catching up: Breus, M. (2013) Can You Ever REALLY Catch-up on Sleep? *Psychology Today: Health, Help, Happiness.*

Exercise study: Oaten, M. & Cheng, K. (2006) Longitudinal Gains in Self-regulation from Regular Physical Exercise. *British Journal of Health Psychology* 11.4: 717-33.

Chapter 4: Strengthening Your Willpower

David Blaine story: Baumeister, R., & Tierney, J. (2011). *Willpower: Rediscovering the greatest human strength.* New York: Penguin Press.

Blaine's first exposure to magic: David Blaine Biography. (2015). *Biography.com* editors.www.biography.com/people/david-blaine-12127585.

Blaine's dedication to magic: David Blaine - Biography. (2015) http://www.all-aboutmagicians.com/davidblaine.html.

Can willpower be strengthened?: Muraven, M., Baumeister, R., & Tice, D. (1999). Longitudinal Improvement of Self-Regulation Through Practice: Building Self-Control Strength Through Repeated Exercise. *The Journal of Social Psychology,* 446-457.

Meditation exercise: Oman, D., Shapiro, S., Thoresen, C., Plante, T., & Flinders, T. (2008). Meditation Lowers Stress And Supports Forgiveness Among College Students: A Randomized Controlled Trial. *Journal of American College Health*, 569-578.

Use your other hand, correct your speech, and meet deadlines exercises: Baumeister, R., Gailliot, M., Dewall, C., & Oaten, M. (2006). Self-Regulation and Personality: How Interventions Increase Regulatory Success, and How Depletion Moderates the Effects of Traits on Behavior. *Journal of Personality*, 1773-1802.

Keep track of your spending exercise: Oaten, M., & Cheng, K. (2007). Improvements in self-control from financial monitoring. *Journal of Economic Psychology*, 487-501.

Squeeze a handgrip exercise: Muraven, M. (2010). Building self-control strength: Practicing self-control leads to improved self-control performance. *Journal of Experimental Social Psychology*, 465-468.

Carry around something tempting exercise: Forman, E., Hoffman, K., Mcgrath, K., Herbert, J., Brandsma, L., & Lowe, M. (2007). A comparison of acceptance- and control-based strategies for coping with food cravings: An analog study. *Behaviour Research and Therapy*, 2372- 2386.

List of successful people who meditate: 3 Famous people who meditate: Transcendental Meditation celebrities - TMhome. (2014, December 10). http://tmhome.com/experiences/famous-people-who-meditate/.

Our wandering mind: Bradt, S. (2010, November 11). Wandering mind not a happy mind.

http://news.harvard.edu/gazette/story/2010/11/wandering-mind-not-a-happymind/.

Meditation increases focus and lowers stress: Brefczynski-Lewis, J., Lutz, A., Schaefer, H., Levinson, D., & Davidson, R. (2007). Neural Correlates Of Attentional Expertise In Long-term Meditation Practitioners. *Proceedings of the National Academy of Sciences,* 11483-11488.

Meditation increases learning ability: Hölzel, B., Carmody, J., Vangel, M., Congleton, C., Yerramsetti, S., Gard, T., & Lazar, S. (2012). Mindfulness practice leads to increases in regional brain gray matter density. *Psychiatry Research: Neuroimaging,* 36-43.

Meditation increases energy: Tang, Y., Lu, Q., Geng, X., Stein, E., Yang, Y., & Posner, M. (2010). Short-Term Meditation Induces White Matter Changes In The Anterior Cingulate. *Proceedings of the National Academy of Sciences,* 15649-15652.

Meditation exercise: Meditation exercise created by Andi Puddicombe of Headspace.com.

How chunking works: Bandura, A., & Schunk, D. (1981). Cultivating Competence, Self-Efficacy, and Intrinsic Interest Through Proximal Self-Motivation. *Journal of Personality and Social Psychology,* 586-598.

Working out for the long-term: McGonigal, Kelly. "Willpower vs. Habit Design." Habit Design® Workshop. San Francisco. Lecture.

Chapter 5: Finding Your Purpose

Arnold Schwarzenegger story: Schwarzenegger, A. (2013). *Total Recall: My Unbelievably True Life Story.* Simon & Schuster.

Quotations and details of Schwarzenegger's time in the military and winning the Junior Mr. Europe: Arnold Schwarzenegger's Amazing Motivational Story. (2012, September 27). https://www.youtube.com/watch?v=wJPRj19OU-w.

Civil Right's Movement information: Duhigg, C. (2012). *The power of habit: Why we do what we do in life and business.* New York: Random House.

How purpose changes perspective: Job, V., Dweck, C. & Walton, G. (2010) Ego Depletion–Is It All in Your Head?: Implicit Theories About Willpower Affect Self-Regulation. *Psychological Science* 21.11 1686-693. Web.

Inspiration increases your want power: Suchy, Y. (2009). Executive Functioning: Overview, Assessment, and Research Issues for Non-Neuropsychologists. *Annals of Behavioral Medicine*, 37(2), 106-116.

The law of attraction: Guinagh, B. (1987). Cognitive Self-Help: Positive Thinking. *Catharsis and Cognition in Psychotherapy*, 81-89.

Positive visualization leads to lack of motivation: Oettingen, G., & Mayer, D. (2002). The motivating function of thinking about the future: Expectations versus fantasies. *Journal of Personality and Social Psychology*, 1198-1212.

Beware of inspiration without action: Fishbach, A., & Dhar, R. (2005). Goals as Excuses or Guides: The Liberating Effect of Perceived Goal Progress on Choice. *Journal of Consumer Research*, 32(3), 370-377.

Confront the brutal facts, but always have faith: Collins, J. C. (2001). *Good to great: Why some companies make the leap--and others don't.* New York, NY: HarperBusiness.

Chapter 6: Becoming Gritty

J.K. Rowling story and quotations: BBC Arts. (2002). J.K. Rowling Biography. https://www.youtube.com/watch?v=Ght2BpCkJYQ.

What is grit?: Duckworth, A. (Apr. 2013) The Key To Success? Grit. Ted Talks. New York. Speech.

The difference between grit and willpower: Duckworth, A. L., Kirby, T. A., Tsukayama, E., Berstein, H., & Ericsson, K. A. (2010). Deliberate Practice Spells Success: Why Grittier Competitors Triumph at the National Spelling Bee. *Social Psychological and Personality Science*, 2(2), 174-181.

Percentage of people who fail their goals in the middle. Statistic Brain. (2015, December 27). http://www.statisticbrain.com/new-years-resolution-statistics/

AA motto of "don't have a drink today": Kaskutas, L. (2009). Alcoholics Anonymous Effectiveness: Faith Meets Science. *Journal of Addictive Diseases*, 145-157.

Jerry Seinfeld story: Clear, J. (2014, January 27). How the 'Seinfeld Strategy' Can Help You Stop Procrastinating. Retrieved from http://www.entrepreneur.com/article/231023.

Value of monitoring your progress: Baumeister, Roy F., and John Tierney. *Willpower: Rediscovering the Greatest Human Strength.* New York: Penguin, 2011.

Chapter 7: Opening Your Mind

Steve Jobs story: Isaacson, W. (2011). *Steve Jobs.* New York: Simon & Schuster.

Daniel Everett story and the dimensional mind: Greene, R. (2013) *Mastery.* New York: Penguin.

How being judgmental affects your brain: Sywelster, R. (2005) The Role of Snap Judgments in Intelligence. *Brain Connection.*

Practicing curiosity strategy: Saville, E. (2014) How Curiosity Changes Our Brains. *The Washington Post.*

Detaching your ego from your ideas and seeking out the unfamiliar strategies: Greene, R. (2013) *Mastery.* New York: Penguin.

Let go of your need to judge and become more mindful of your daily decisions strategies: Kahneman, D. (2011). *Thinking, fast and slow.* New York: Farrar, Straus and Giroux.

Steve Jobs triumphant return story: Collins, J., & Hansen, M. (2011). *Great by choice: Uncertainty, chaos, and luck: Why some thrive despite them all.* New York, NY: HarperCollins.

Steve Jobs quote about Apple as a sinking ship: Jobs, S. (1997). Steve Jobs Funniest Joke. Even Bill Gates Laughs! https://www.youtube.com/watch?v=Qv1pvRDFFqs

Chapter 8: Overcoming Limits

Jure Robic story: Coyle, D. (2006) That Which Does Not Kill Me Makes Me Stranger. *The New York Times.* Web. http://www.nytimes.com/2006/02/05/sports/playmagazine/05robicpm.html

Inferences about the science of fatigue and willpower: McGonigal, K. (2012). *The willpower instinct: How self-control works, why it matters, and what you can do to get more of it.* New York: Avery.

Original study on fatigue: Hill, A., Long, C. & Lupton, H. (1924) Muscular Exercise, Lactic Acid, and the Supply and Utilisation of Oxygen. *Proceedings of the Royal Society B: Biological Sciences* 96.679 438-75.

Later study concluding that fatigue is an emotion: Noakes, D. (2005) From Catastrophe to Complexity: A Novel Model of Integrative Central Neural Regulation of Effort and Fatigue during Exercise in Humans: Summary and Conclusions. *British Journal of Sports Medicine* 39.2.

The limits of willpower: Job, V., Dweck, C., & Walton, G. (2010) Ego Depletion—Is It All in Your Head?: Implicit Theories About Willpower Affect Self-Regulation. *Psychological Science* 21.11 1686-693.

Story of Brent: This Guy Had An Embarrassing Day At The Gym - So Arnold Schwarzenegger Gave Him A Pep Talk. (2015, March 22) http://broscience.co/embarrasing-day-at-gym-arnold-pep-talk/.

Nelson Mandela courage quote: Mandela, N. (1994). *Long walk to freedom: The autobiography of Nelson Mandela.* Boston: Little, Brown.

Why we fear being vulnerable: Dunbar, R.i.m. (2003) TSB: Mind, Language, and Society in Evolutionary Perspective. *Annual Review of Anthropology* 32.1: 163-81.

Your best friend will give you better advice than you will give yourself: Heath, C., & Heath, D. (2013). *Decisive.* New York: Crown Business.

The comfort/chaos/learning zone concepts: Colvin, G. (2008). *Talent is overrated: What really separates world-class performers from everybody else.* New York: Portfolio.

The learning zone sweet spot: Coyle, D. (2009). *The talent code: Greatness isn't born: It's grown, here's how.* New York: Bantam Books.

Chapter 9: The Long Term

Warren Buffett story: Schroeder, A. (2008). *The snowball: Warren Buffett and the business of life.* New York: Bantam Books.

Summary of Security Analysis: Graham, B., & Dodd, D. (1988). *Graham and Dodd's security analysis (5th ed.).* New York: McGraw-Hill.

Buffett quote about being "hardwired since birth to allocate capital": Colvin, G. (2008). *Talent is overrated: What really separates world-class performers from everybody else.* New York: Portfolio.

Yahoo Finance quote about Buffett's strategy: Riley, D., & Yangala, V. (2013, December 25). *Warren Buffett's secrets, our 10 favorite quotes & one you won't find.* http://finance.yahoo.com/news/warren-buffett-secrets-10-favorite-194528953.html

The Snowball concept: Olson, J., & Mann, J. (2013). *The slight edge (8th anniversary ed.).* Austin, TX: Greenleaf Book Group Press.

The over-ambitious exercisers study: Zauberman, G., & Lynch, J. G. (2005). Resource Slack and Propensity to Discount Delayed Investments of Time versus Money. *SSRN Electronic Journal.*

The planning fallacy study: Buehler, R., Griffin, D., & Ross, M. (1994). Exploring the "planning fallacy": Why people underestimate their task completion times. *Journal of Personality and Social Psychology, 67(3),* 366-381.

Examples of being too optimistic: Sharot, T. (2012). The Optimism Bias. Speech presented at Ted Talks, Long Beach.

Reference class forecasting: Flyvbjerg, B. (2008). Curbing Optimism Bias and Strategic Misrepresentation in Planning: Reference Class Forecasting in Practice. European Planning Studies European Planning Stud. *CEPS,* 16(1), 3-21.

Impulsiveness and delay discounting cause procrastination: Baumeister, R., & Tierney, J. (2011). *Willpower: Rediscovering the greatest human strength.* New York: Penguin Press.

Perfectionism causes procrastination: Steel, P. (2007). The Nature Of Procrastination: A Meta-analytic And Theoretical Review Of Quintessential Self-regulatory Failure. *Psychological Bulletin,* 65-94.

People will choose $50 today rather than $100 a month from now: Madden, G. J., Begotka, A. M., Raiff, B. R., & Kastern, L. L. (2003). Delay discounting of real and hypothetical rewards. *Experimental and Clinical Psychopharmacology, 11(2), 139-145.*

Study of college students who procrastinate: Tice, D., & Baumeister, R. (1997). Longitudinal Study of Procrastination, Performance, Stress and Health: The Costs And Benefits Of Dawdling. *Psychological Science,* 454-458.

Imagining future physical exertion causes fatigue: Noakes, D. (2005) From Catastrophe to Complexity: A Novel Model of Integrative Central Neural Regulation of Effort and Fatigue during Exercise in Humans: Summary and Conclusions. *British Journal of Sports Medicine* 39.2.

Imagining future rewards causes a release of dopamine: Berridge, K. (2006). The debate over dopamine's role in reward: The case for incentive salience. *Psychopharmacology*, 391-431.

Your brain burns glucose as you envision future options: Vohs, K., Baumeister, R., Schmeichel, B., Twenge, J., Nelson, N., & Tice, D. (2008) Making Choices Impairs Subsequent Self-control: A Limited-resource Account of Decision Making, Self-regulation, and Active Initiative. *Journal of Personality and Social Psychology* 94.5: 883-98.

Meditation trains your mind to stay in the present: Oman, D., Shapiro, S., Thoresen, C., Plante, T., & Flinders, T. (2008). Meditation Lowers Stress And Supports Forgiveness Among College Students: A Randomized Controlled Trial. *Journal of American College Health*, 569-578.

Chapter 10: The Pursuit of Perfection

Vince Lombardi story: Maraniss, D. (1999). *When pride still mattered: A life of Vince Lombardi.* New York, NY: Simon & Schuster.

Quotes by Green Bay Packer players and details of Lombardi's struggle to get a coaching job: Vince Lombardi: A Football Life [Motion picture on Documentary]. (2011). United States: NFL Network.

Steven Covey quote about principles: Miller, S. (2009, January 16). Q & A with Dr. Stephen R. Covey. Retrieved May 13, 2015, http://www.franklincovey.com/blog/dr-stephen-covey.html.

Value of objectivity in determining your principles: Why we justify settling: A theory of objective self awareness. Duval, Shelley; Wicklund, Robert A. Oxford, England: *Academic Press.* (1972). 238.

How principles will help you bring out the best version of yourself: Baumeister, Roy F., and John Tierney. *Willpower: Rediscovering the Greatest Human Strength.* New York: Penguin, 2011.

The internal locus of control: Horn, T. (2008). *Advances in sport psychology (3rd ed.).* Champaign, IL: Human Kinetics.

Chapter 11: The Next Generation

Temple Grandin story: Grandin, T. (2006). *Thinking in pictures: And other reports from my life with autism.* Vintage; Reissue edition.

The perspective of Grandin acquiring mastery: Greene, R. (2012). *Mastery.* New York: Viking.

Study on the consequences of artificially boosting self-esteem: Crocker, J. (2002). The Costs of Seeking Self-Esteem. *Journal of Social Issues J Social Issues,* 58(3), 597-615.

Statistics on alcohol, drug use, and obesity in children with boosted self-esteem: Paulhus, D. L. (1998). Interpersonal and intrapsychic adaptiveness of trait self-enhancement: A mixed blessing? *Journal of Personality and Social Psychology,* 74(5), 1197-1208.

Study on self-esteem boosts to attempt to improve midterm grades: Paulhus, D. L. (1998). Interpersonal and intrapsychic adaptiveness of trait self-enhancement: A mixed blessing? *Journal of Personality and Social Psychology,* 74(5), 1197-1208.

The longitudinal study of the marshmallow test: Mischel, W., Ayduk, O., Berman, M. G., Casey, B. J., Gotlib, I. H., Jonides, J., . . . Shoda, Y. (2010). 'Willpower' over the life span: Decomposing self-regulation. *Social Cognitive and Affective Neuroscience,* 6(2), 252-256.

Raising children with strong willpower strategies: Baumeister, R., & Tierney, J. (2011). *Willpower: Rediscovering the greatest human strength.* New York: Penguin Press.

Asian parenting style of preaching large, long-term rewards: Abboud, S., & Kim, J. (2005) *Top of the class: how Asian parents raise high achievers—and you can too.* New York: Berkley Books.

John Wooden story: Wooden, J., & Jamison, S. (2005). *Wooden on leadership.* New York: McGraw-Hill.

Learning through failure: Taleb, N. N. (2012). *Antifragile: Things that gain from disorder.* New York: Random House.

Chapter 12: The Journey without an End

Alex Kleiner story: Facts and quotations are drawn from interviews with Kleiner.

Losing a battle: BBC Arts. (2002). J.K. Rowling Biography. https://www.youtube.com/watch?v=Ght2BpCkJYQ.

Settling for good: Isaacson, W. (2011). *Steve Jobs.* New York: Simon & Schuster.

Index

The Will of Heroes

The Proven Path to Greatness That Anyone Can Follow

Colin Robertson

Learn more about your willpower at www.willpowered.co